MR 19 '96

WITHDRAWN FROM
Dickinson Public Library

747.3 F

D0852553

Picture-perfect walls

MR 19 '96

Arts & Crafts for ▢ Home Decorating®

PICTURE-PERFECT WALLS

Techniques & Ideas for Framing, Matting & Wall Arrangements

DICKINSON AREA PUBLIC
LIBRARY
139 Third Street West
Dickinson, North Dakota 58601

The Home Decorating Institute®

Copyright © 1995 Cy DeCosse Incorporated 5900 Green Oak Drive Minnetonka, Minnesota 55343
1-800-328-3895 All rights reserved Printed in U.S.A.

Library of Congress Cataloging-in-Publication Data Picture-perfect walls / The Home Decorating Institute. p. cm. — (Arts &
crafts for home decorating) Includes index. ISBN 0-86573-378-3 (hardcover) — ISBN 0-86573-379-1 (softcover) 1. Walls.
2. Interior decoration. I. Home Decorating Institute (Minnetonka, Minn.) II. Series. NK2119.P52 1995 747'.3—dc20
95-30809

CONTENTS

Wall Arrangements & Display Basics

Matting & Framing

Creative Framing Ideas

Floral Accessories

Decorative Shelves

WALL ARRANGEMENTS

Artful wall displays are the finishing touches that add interest and personality to rooms. Make your wall arrangements unique with customized mats and frames, floral accessories, and decorative shelves.

Enhance flat artwork, needle-art projects, and dimensional items, such as coins or pressed flowers, with custom-cut mats. Embellish mats with flourishes or marbleized paper for added distinction.

Create one-of-a-kind frames to complement your pictures and photographs. Select from frames embellished with paper, metal, or decorative bundles. Or use spray enamel paints to make elegant marbleized frames.

Add color and texture to a wall with a floral display. Complement a picture or embellish a narrow wall space with a swag or a trio of wall bundles. For variety, make a wall basket arrangement or mantel arrangement that reflects the season.

Shelves add dimensional interest and can be used to display pictures and collectibles. Select from tiered shelves, rustic-style shelves, and custom-size wall boxes.

All information in this book has been tested; however, because skill levels and conditions vary, the publisher disclaims any liability for unsatisfactory results. Follow the manufacturers' instructions for tools and materials used to complete these projects. The publisher is not responsible for any injury or damage caused by the improper use of tools, materials, or information in this publication.

WALL DISPLAYS

Hand-woven rug *is the focal point of this grouping; hang the rug as on page 31. The basket and the masks add dimensional interest to the display. The frame with decorative bundles (page 76) displays a nature photograph.*

For interest and variety in wall displays, combine flat artwork with three-dimensional pieces. When selecting display pieces, consider how they can be used with artwork and decorative objects you already own. Wall displays that incorporate collections and memorabilia make the most personal statement.

Quilt *is framed with a raised mat (page 53). Collectible dishes sit on rustic shelves (page 118), adding dimensional interest.*

Sheet music and instrument *are creatively displayed with a collection of pictures. The crown molding shelves (page 122) are ideal display ledges for pictures. Enhance a picture frame with a marbleized finish as on page 74.*

Mat with multiple openings *(page 48) displays childhood photos. The tiered shelf (page 114) contains a collection of toys and a child's drawing. Artwork is displayed in a multiple mat (page 44).*

WALL DISPLAYS
(CONTINUED)

Birdcage *(page 100) is displayed with botanical prints. The prints are highlighted with mats embellished with marbleized paper (page 56).*

Single mats *(page 36) are used to frame a collection of nature prints and pressed leaves. The nature prints in the center combine the techniques for single mats with irregular openings (page 36) and mats with multiple openings (page 48).*

Mirror with floral accents (page 90) is displayed above a dressing table. Small prints have mats embellished with rub-on lines (page 56). The prints are hung on each side of the mirror, using decorative hangers (page 84).

Wall boxes (page 108) display a collection of vintage dolls and toys.

DISPLAYS FOR UNIQUE SPACES

Wall groupings in unique spaces, such as stairways, corners, and above windows or doors, are often the displays that bring a sense of originality to a home. These displays can highlight an architectural feature, add an element of surprise, or call attention to small pieces of artwork that might otherwise go unnoticed.

When displaying artwork in unique areas, be sure that the display is in proportion to the wall space and that it is positioned at the correct height. You may want to experiment, using paper patterns as on page 28, to avoid rehanging items. If the display is not positioned above furniture and does not appear anchored, try placing a chair, stool, or plant beneath the arrangement.

Wall along a staircase (right) has a stair-step arrangement of artwork to keep the images at eye level.

Space above a bookcase (below) features elements displayed both on the wall and on the bookcase. A small lamp illuminates the grouping.

Narrow wall space *highlights a pair of pictures anchored by a pedestal.*

Wall above a window *is the perfect space for a display of fishing memorabilia.*

MANTEL & SHELF DISPLAYS

Mantels, and the wall spaces above them, are traditional places for displaying pictures. The fireplace is often the focal point in a room, and anything displayed above it receives immediate attention.

Display dimensional objects on the mantel to complement the artwork displayed on the wall. Vary the height of the items for a more interesting arrangement. Small frames can be placed on easels. Collectibles can be displayed on books or boxes to vary the height. Avoid placing objects in a row, since overlapped or staggered arrangements are more interesting to view. Unless you are arranging a formal, symmetrical display, an unequal number of collectibles usually makes a more pleasing arrangement.

Collection of architectural prints (below) is arranged above the mantel. The candlesticks and collectibles displayed on the mantel repeat the theme.

Framed map (above) is displayed on the front of a shelf. Mounting pieces included with the metal frame kit secure the map to picture hangers attached to the shelf at each side of the frame.

Whether built-in or freestanding, bookcases and buffet shelves offer perfect display areas. Shelving can be both practical and decorative when favorite collectibles and artwork are arranged among the functional items.

Add interest to shelves by creating a mix of textures, colors, and shapes. Break up the background of stored books by propping pictures or collectibles in front of them. Alternate stacking methods, and display books with colorful covers face front.

Display dishes in groupings for impact, overlapping pieces for depth. Mix in linens to soften the look, and tuck in framed pictures, baskets, or plants for additional texture.

Experiment with different arrangements until there is a smooth visual flow of objects. Each shelf should have its own arrangement and focal point, with the entire shelving unit having an overall unified look.

Display of kitchen accessories (above) includes functional bowls and cookbooks, as well as decorative bottles, vegetable prints, and antique utensils.

Botanical prints (below) are artfully arranged with a carved relief, sconce, and mirror. Vase with tulips fills in the bare area beneath the sconce, balancing the wall grouping.

LIGHTING

Lighting brings special emphasis to artwork and adds drama to the room. Lighting can also be used to make artwork displayed in less prominent or dark areas of a room more visible.

A variety of lighting sources can be used to highlight artwork. Table lamps and overhead lighting will often sufficiently illuminate artwork hung over furniture. Track lighting or recessed lighting works well to spotlight pieces that are focal points in a room. Additional accent lighting sources, such as uplights and sconces, can also be used to cast soft lighting on displays. For special pictures, you may want to mount a picture lamp above the artwork. In general, the length of this style lamp should be about two-thirds the width of the picture.

When hanging artwork, consider how you can use existing light sources to enhance displays; then determine if additional lighting sources are desired. For example, you may want to plan a wall display to take advantage of recessed spotlights installed in a room. When lighting groupings of artwork, you do not need to light the entire grouping. You may want to spotlight focal pieces, or call attention to small pieces that might be overlooked without lighting.

For lighting that closely resembles natural daylight, use halogen bulbs. Avoid highlighting artwork with fluorescent bulbs, since fluorescent bulbs emit UV rays that can be damaging to artwork.

Wall sconce, *displayed within an asymmetrical wall grouping, draws attention to the wall display and provides mood lighting.*

Track lighting has individual canisters, positioned to spotlight dominant pieces in a mantel grouping.

Uplight (left), concealed behind a chair, illuminates a collection of masks. The tilt-style design of the lamp allows the direction of the light to be adjusted.

Picture lamp (right), mounted behind the frame, illuminates a special print.

Lighting tube (below), mounted under a shelf, casts soft lighting on a collection of family photographs.

Display Basics

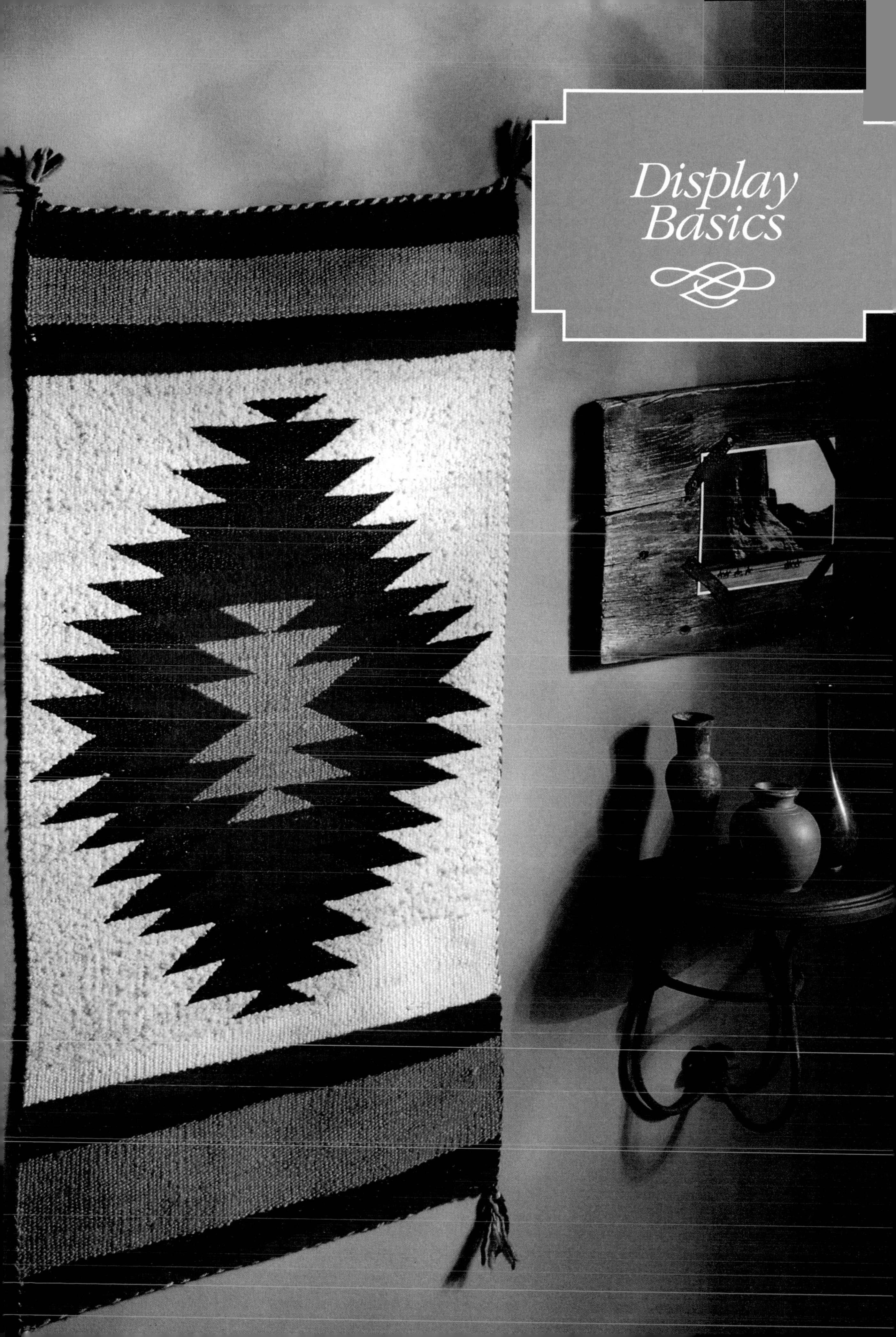

DESIGN BASICS

Whether you are displaying flat artwork or three-dimensional items, following some basic design guidelines for unity, balance, proportion, color, and pattern will help you display artwork successfully.

Select artwork and accessories that reflect the mood of the room. Botanical prints emphasize the floral charm of traditional English country, while bold graphic prints complement the dramatic and streamlined styling of a contemporary decor.

When selecting the location for a wall grouping, consider the direction from which the grouping will be viewed, as well as any focal points in the room. Areas above large pieces of furniture, such as sofas, buffets, and beds, are natural choices for wall displays. Take into account how furniture and other objects positioned against a wall become part of the wall grouping. Also consider hanging artwork on the wall spaces opposite entryways. Hallways are ideal for displaying small, detailed art pieces, which are best viewed up close. Large pictures require more space for

Symmetrical arrangements have elements that are positioned identically on each side of the arrangement. Right, small shelves display statues on each side of a mirror. Above, sconces highlight a pair of companion prints.

viewing; therefore, they are best displayed where they can be viewed from a distance.

Hang artwork at eye level, taking into account whether it will be viewed from a standing or sitting position. In general, the space between a piece of furniture and a framed piece of artwork should not be more than 4" to 7" (10 to 18 cm). When hanging shelves and baskets or other dimensional items, be sure they are positioned high enough so no one will bump into them.

BALANCE

Wall arrangements can be displayed either symmetrically or asymmetrically. Symmetrical arrangements are identical on either side from the center of the display. This type of arrangement is used for a formal, traditional look. Asymmetrical groupings, when divided down the center, have two halves that look different; however, the grouping is balanced, because the visual weight on both sides is the same.

Asymmetrical arrangements have elements that are arranged differently on each side of the display. Left, shelves with decorative vases are grouped with a plate on one side of a tapestry. Above, pictures in various sizes are combined with wood medallions and a mirror.

Large, single rectangular picture is in proportion to the furniture below it.

PROPORTION

For proper proportion, the size of a wall grouping should relate in size to its surroundings. Generally, it is best to place a large display in a large space and a small display in a small space. A large display may consist of a single large item, such as a print, rug, or quilt, or it may consist of a grouping of several small items.

Unless a picture or grouping is very large, it usually needs a piece of furniture to *anchor* it, or give it a sense of belonging. In general, wall displays should not extend beyond the boundaries of the furniture positioned against the wall below.

To make a small print or picture correctly proportioned for a large space, frame it with a wide multiple mat or a wide frame molding to increase its size. In contrast, a large print can be visually reduced in size by using a narrow frame molding with a mat that blends with the wall color.

Picture and plant *displayed above a chair are in proportion to the width of the chair back.*

Kitchen utensils and baking pieces *(opposite) are grouped with pictures to make a display that is in proportion to the side table below.*

COLOR

Bold wall grouping *is created by displaying artwork that repeats the colors found in the accessories.*

When selecting artwork for wall groupings, consider the colors in the room, including the colors of the walls, fabrics, and carpet. Dark, heavy pictures and accessories placed on light-colored walls will often appear spotty. Dark-colored walls are generally easier to work with and can have light or dark groupings. For soft, subtle wall displays, choose colors that are harmonious to the room. For bolder displays, incorporate accent colors into wall arrangements. Bold colors in wall displays, that repeat the colors of accessories, such as rugs or pillows, create visual movement and a livelier atmosphere.

When framing artwork, also consider the effect the colors have on the style and the visual size of the picture. Pictures in high-contrast mats or frames appear visually larger than artwork framed for low contrast.

Colors of mats and frames *influence the style and visual size of the picture. Near right, the warm gold mat tones and frame lend a traditional look to the picture. In the center photo, the deep red mat and black frame draw the eye into the picture, visually reducing its size. On the far right, the picture takes on a contemporary look, with a neutral mat and a sleek metal frame. The lighter mat and frame visually increase the size of the picture.*

Subtle, harmonious wall grouping *repeats the colors of the furnishings.*

PATTERN

When displaying pictures or artwork on patterned walls, it is important that the artwork does not compete for attention. Choose artwork in harmonious colors and patterns that will not appear too busy on the wall. In order for framed artwork to stand out, consider using a wide mat or frame to help establish the boundaries of the picture. Accessories such as mirrors, plants, sconces, and solid-colored plates can add dimension and interest without appearing too busy.

Mirrors *(right) embellish a patterned traditional wallcovering.*

Solid-colored dinnerware
*(above), displayed on a wall
shelf, adds interest to a wall
without distracting from the
wallcovering pattern.*

Delicate print *(left)
harmonizes with the
wallcovering. The plaster
relief designs add depth
to the grouping.*

UNITY

Grouping miscellaneous pieces of artwork together requires careful consideration in order for the pieces to appear as though they belong together. Unrelated pieces can be unified by similarity of mat and frame style, color, subject matter, size of artwork, and artist's medium.

Different-size photos (above) *are unified in a display of three identical-size frames by varying the size of the image openings.*

Grouping of botanical prints (opposite) *is a unified display because of the similarity of the subject matter, even though the mat and frame styles vary.*

Collection of sports memorabilia *is displayed together to create a unified grouping.*

PICTURE GROUPINGS

Groupings of pictures provide visual interest and can be used to fill large wall spaces or to call attention to a unique space. Small pictures will have more impact displayed together than if displayed separately around the room.

For unique wall displays, combine accessories with a variety of shapes and textures. Plates can add both color and depth. Wall shelves can be used to display sculptures and other collectibles. Items such as bellpulls, baskets, and rugs provide additional interest.

The wall display should be contained within the dimensions of the furniture below it. Arrange items so as a group they form a shape such as a rectangle,

Experiment with the placement of items in a grouping, using paper patterns. Temporarily secure paper patterns to the wall using removable tape or poster putty. Mark the placement positions lightly with a pencil.

oval, or triangle. This helps give the grouping a unified appearance.

In general, position large pictures low, and group similar sizes and shapes together. Pay attention to the spacing between pieces; if the space is too narrow, the pictures will lose their individuality. If there is too much space between the pieces of artwork, the grouping will not appear cohesive.

Before hanging a grouping, experiment by arranging the pieces on the floor until the display is pleasing to the eye. To get the proper visual perspective, make paper patterns and tape them to the wall.

TIPS FOR PICTURE GROUPINGS

Arrange frames and dimensional items so there is at least one strong vertical line or one strong horizontal line in the grouping.

Position light and dark artwork so it is balanced throughout the grouping.

Place a straight-lined piece at each end of the grouping; keep shaped items toward the center.

Use groupings of small pictures to help balance a large picture.

Position the grouping so the midpoint is at eye level.

Use vertical arrangements to emphasize or add visual height to a room; use horizontal arrangements to emphasize or add visual width to a room.

Rectangular grouping *combines several pieces of square and rectangular artwork.*

Triangular grouping *is achieved by arranging framed needlework in a stair-step manner.*

Oval grouping *incorporates oval and diamond shapes to help create the silhouette.*

HANGING ARTWORK

A variety of methods can be used for hanging artwork, depending on whether you are hanging framed artwork or three-dimensional items. As a precaution, when hanging heavy objects, secure the mounting hardware into a wall stud.

HOW TO HANG A PICTURE

MATERIALS

- Metal tape measure.
- Pencil.
- Picture hanger, in appropriate size for weight of picture; nail.
- Hammer.
- Carpenter's level.

1 **Small or lightweight picture.** Determine placement of the picture; mark the wall at the center of the top of the frame.

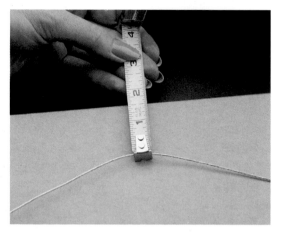

2 Pull the picture wire on the back of the frame taut, using a metal tape measure; record distance from the wire to the top of the frame.

3 Measure down from mark on wall the distance determined in step 2; mark an X. Position picture hanger so bottom of the hanger is at the X; secure with a nail.

4 Hang picture; straighten, using a carpenter's level.

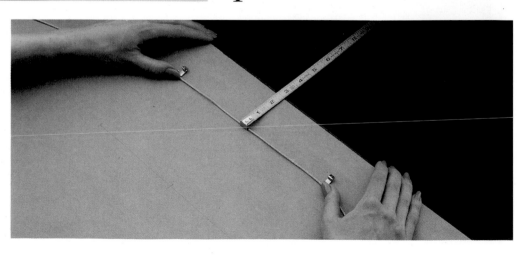

1 **Large or heavy picture.** Follow steps 1 and 2 above, pulling the wire taut with two picture hangers as shown. Record half the distance between picture hangers. Mark an X as in step 3. Measure from the X the distance just recorded, to mark placement for a hanger on each side of X. Complete as in steps 3 and 4.

TIPS FOR HANGING ARTWORK

Spring-tension plate hangers, available in a variety of sizes, are used for displaying decorative plates. For best protection, purchase hangers with plastic-coated ends or adjust the ends with pliers as necessary to avoid scratching the finish on the plate.

Carpet tacking strip, mounted to a wall, can be used to hang heavy, textured rugs. Cut tacking strip slightly shorter than the width of rug, and hang it with the pins angled toward the ceiling.

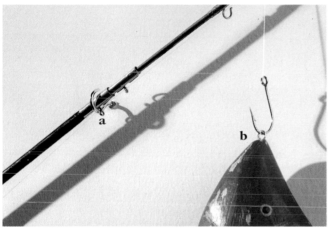

Support hooks and screw eyes can be used to hang three-dimensional items. Support hooks **(a)** hold a fishing rod in place; screw eye **(b)** is inserted into a wooden fish to make it suitable for displaying on a fishhook.

Silicone glue can be used for mounting lightweight items to the wall. Support items with pieces of masking tape until glue is set.

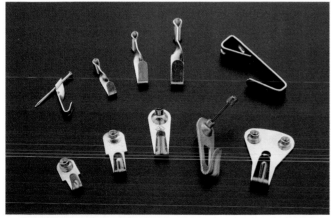

Picture hangers, available in a variety of sizes, are used for hanging framed artwork. Picture hangers distribute the weight of the picture more evenly than a single nail and are less likely to pull out of the wall.

Nail holes in wallcovering will be less noticeable if positioned over a design motif rather than on the background.

Matting
& Framing

MATTING & FRAMING BASICS

Learn matting and framing techniques in order to create distinctive displays for artwork and memorabilia at substantial savings. Turn items as simple as greeting cards or postcards into artwork.

A single mat is often all that is needed to enhance a print or photograph. For more creative displays, cut specialty mats, such as multiple mats (page 44) or mats with multiple openings (page 48). Or frame dimensional items using raised mats (page 53). Depending on the type of artwork, a variety of mounting techniques (pages 39 to 41) are used. After cutting the mat and mounting the artwork, you can easily assemble the picture and frame (pages 42 and 43).

FRAME SELECTION

Choose a frame style that is correctly proportioned and that complements the artwork, taking into consideration where the picture will be displayed. Be sure the frame can support the weight of the glass and has the correct mounting space for the thickness of the mats and backing.

In many cases, you may be able to use a preassembled, standard-size frame. Unassembled frames, in a variety of styles, are sold in packages containing two sides and are available in 1" (2.5 cm) increments. Sides of different lengths can be combined for a greater variety of sizes. For special displays, you may want to consider ordering a custom frame.

MATTING & FRAMING SUPPLIES

Matting supplies are often available at art supply stores and custom framing shops. Mat boards **(a)** can be found in a wide variety of colors and textures, including silk, marble, linen, and suede. There are two basic types of mat boards: paper and rag. Paper mats, often referred to as acid-free mats, have been buffered to neutralize the acid in the wood pulp; the core, however, is not acid free and will discolor over time. Rag mats, or conservation-quality mats, are the highest grade and do not contain any wood pulp. These mats offer the greatest protection and are recommended for artwork with monetary or sentimental value.

Use a mat cutter **(b)** that cuts a 45° beveled edge. Mat cutters are available in a variety of styles and prices. For best results, select one that has a retractable blade and is marked with a start-and-stop line. Specific cutting instructions may vary with the type of mat cutter. The cutting instructions in this book are for a mat cutter that is pulled toward you. If your mat cutter is designed to be pushed away from you, reverse the cutting instructions.

For accurate measuring, use a metal straightedge **(c)** with 1/16" (1.5 mm) markings, for cutting mat boards and mounting boards. For best results, choose a straightedge with a rubber or cork backing to prevent slipping, a major cause of cutting inaccuracies. A T-square **(d)** is helpful for ensuring square mats and backing boards.

Use specialty tapes to ensure professional results. Adhesive transfer gum tape **(e),** often called ATG tape, has many applications in framing. This acid-neutral double-stick transfer tape is easy to work with and does not deteriorate with age. This is often the only tape needed for matting and framing inexpensive artwork. Framer's tapes are used for mounting artwork of monetary or sentimental value. These acid-free tapes are available in self-adhesive **(f)** and gummed **(g)** varieties. For the best protection, select an archival-quality tape. Some art supply stores and framing shops will sell framer's tapes in short lengths. Avoid using transparent tape or masking tape; these tapes may lose adhesive quality over time and cause photographs or prints to yellow.

A backing board prevents a print or photograph from warping. Foam-core board **(h)** is a lightweight, acid-neutral backing board. It is available in 1/8" and 3/16" (3 mm and 4.5 mm) thicknesses. Heavyweight ply board is also sometimes used as a backing board. Standard mat board can be used as a backing board in frames measuring 11" × 14" (28 × 35.5 cm) or smaller.

Hardware stores supply and cut single-strength glass **(i),** an inexpensive and distortion-free glass suitable for most artwork. For valuable items, you may want to use a UV-protective glass. Available at framing shops, this glass provides protection from the sun's damaging ultraviolet rays.

BASIC TECHNIQUES

When cutting mats and backing boards, measure the inside mounting space of the frame, and cut the backing and outer mat board 1/8" (3 mm) smaller; also have the glass cut to this dimension. This fitting ease allows for expansion due to humidity. If you are ordering a custom frame, the fitting ease will be allowed when the frame is cut. Order the frame, specifying the exact size of the backing and outer mat board.

For accurate measuring, mark mats using a very sharp, hard lead pencil. To ensure clean beveled cuts, always place a scrap piece of mat under the area to be cut and replace blades frequently.

SINGLE MATS

Single mats can be made in three styles. For a basic single mat (above, right), cut a square or rectangular opening. For additional interest, cut an image opening with offset corners (above). Or, for a unique, nontraditional look, cut an angular, nonrectangular opening (right).

Select a mat board that enhances the colors in the artwork. Usually, a single or outer mat repeats one of the dominant colors in the picture or blends with the colors in the artwork. A mat color that is stronger than the colors of the artwork draws attention away from the artwork.

The width of the mat border on a single mat varies, depending on the size of the artwork and the desired look. As a general rule, make the mat width at least twice the width of the frame molding. For frames 20" × 24" (51 × 61 cm) or larger, cut the mat border at least three times the width of the frame molding. In many cases, all four borders of the mat are equal in width. Contemporary prints, however, often have mats with unequal borders. If desired, the lower border of the mat may be cut wider than the other three to create visual weight.

In order to accurately cut the image opening, start with an accurately cut, squared board. Unless the edges of the artwork will be exposed, such as on artwork with a torn or deckled edge, cut the image opening at least ¼" (6 mm) smaller than the dimensions of the artwork.

MATERIALS

- Mat board.
- Mat cutter; utility knife.
- Hard-lead, sharp pencil.
- Metal straightedge with rubber or cork backing.
- Metal nail file; artist's burnisher.
- Tracing paper, for angular, nonrectangular opening.

HOW TO CUT A BASIC SINGLE MAT

1 Mark outside dimensions of mat on wrong side of mat board, taking care to mark square corners. Using a utility knife and straightedge, score along marked lines; repeat until board is cut through.

2 Mark the width of mat borders on wrong side of mat board, measuring from each edge; make two marks on each side. Using a sharp pencil and a straightedge, draw lines connecting the marks.

3 Place a scrap of mat board under the area to be cut. Using straightedge, align edge of mat cutter with marked line, placing the start-and-stop line (arrow) of cutter even with upper border line.

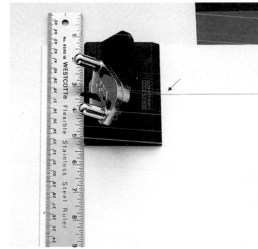

4 Push blade into mat. Cut on marked line in one smooth pass; stop when start-and-stop line (arrow) meets lower border line. Pull the blade out of mat. Rotate the board 90°, and cut adjacent side; repeat to cut remaining sides.

5 Remove center piece, or fallout; if a corner is cut short, insert a single-edge razor blade, aligning angle of blade with bevel. Gently slide blade toward corner until fallout is released.

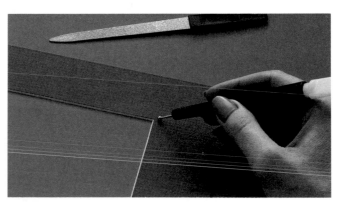

6 Smooth ragged beveled edge, if necessary, using a nail file. On face side of mat, smooth overcuts by lightly rubbing mat with tip of burnisher; this makes overcut less noticeable.

HOW TO CUT A SINGLE MAT WITH OFFSET CORNERS

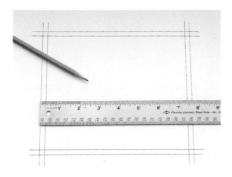

1 Cut and mark the mat board as on page 37, steps 1 and 2. Mark a parallel line ¼" (6 mm) in from each marked line, extending lines beyond image opening.

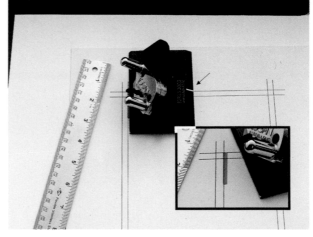

2 Align edge of mat cutter with straightedge, along inside marked line, placing start-and-stop line (arrow) of cutter even with the outer marked line. Push blade into mat. Cut ¼" (6 mm) offset; line can be overcut, extending into the center area of mat. Highlighted line (inset) shows detail of cut. Rotate the board, and repeat at each corner.

3 Reposition the board to cut remaining offset line at each corner; start cut in center area of image opening, and stop when start-and-stop line of cutter is even with outer marked line.

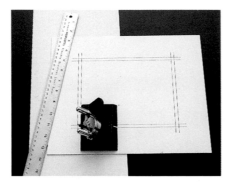

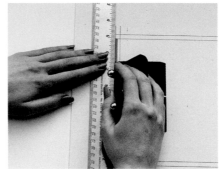

4 Complete the mat as on page 37, steps 3 to 6, aligning the edge of the mat cutter with outer marked lines; align start-and-stop line of the cutter with inner marked lines.

HOW TO CUT A SINGLE MAT WITH AN ANGULAR OPENING

1 Cut the mat as on page 37, step 1. Mark the desired image opening on the tracing paper, using a pencil. Place the paper over artwork, checking for accuracy; re-mark image opening as necessary.

2 Turn the paper over, and position as desired on back of the mat board. Retrace image opening on the marked lines to transfer to mat board. Mark lines at each corner, perpendicular to each side of the image opening, for aligning the mat cutter.

3 Cut the mat as on page 37, steps 3 to 6; align start-and-stop line of the cutter with marked guidelines as shown. Rotate mat as necessary to cut each adjacent line.

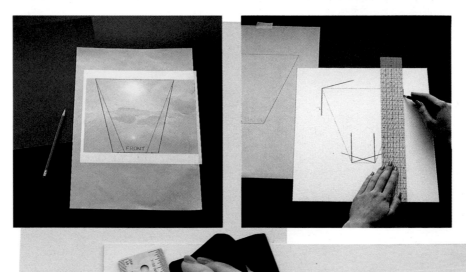

MOUNTING TECHNIQUES

There are a variety of mounting techniques that may be used for securing artwork for framing. When selecting a method, take into consideration the item being mounted, the mat style, and the value of the item being framed.

Hinge mounting is the preferred technique for securing flat pieces of artwork. Depending on the mat style, use one of two methods for hinge mounting. If the image opening of the mat is smaller than the size of the artwork, then the artwork is hinged to the back of the mat board and the backing board is placed behind the picture. If the edges of the artwork are exposed within the image opening of the mat, the picture is hinged to a mounting board. Inexpensive items, such as greeting cards and postcards, can be mounted directly to a mounting board, using double-stick transfer tape.

Artwork may also be dry-mounted at a custom framing shop. This permanent type of mounting is especially recommended for lightweight prints, such as posters, that have a tendency to bubble or ripple.

Most dimensional items can be glued or stitched in place. When using stitches to mount items such as textiles or small pieces of jewelry, choose a thread that matches the item. Or use monofilament fishing line.

Some items, such as coins or dried flowers, can be secured in place using silicone glue or a hot glue gun and glue sticks. Clear silicone glue, available at hardware stores, is the preferred method for valuable or sentimental items. This glue stays flexible and can be removed without damaging the item.

A colored mat board is often used for mounting dimensional items and flat artwork with exposed edges. To prevent the mounting board from warping, especially on large framed artwork, a backing board is recommended.

MATERIALS

- Mat board.
- Utility knife; metal straightedge with rubber or cork backing.
- Backing board, such as foam-core board or heavyweight ply board.
- Mounting board, for hinge mounting to a mounting board and for mounting with glue or hand stitches.
- Framer's tape, for hinge mounting.
- Silicone glue or hot glue gun and glue sticks, for mounting with glue.
- Thread, T-pin, and awl, for mounting with hand stitches.

HOW TO HINGE-MOUNT ARTWORK TO A MAT

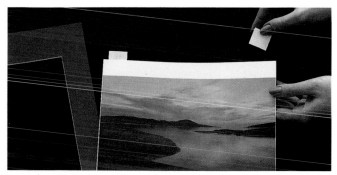

1 Cut mat as desired. Place the picture, faceup, on a smooth surface. Cut two strips of framer's tape, each about 1" (2.5 cm) long; secure one-half the length of each strip to back upper edge of artwork as shown.

2 Place the mat, faceup, over artwork, in desired position. Press firmly along upper border of mat to secure the tape. If using gummed framer's tape, moisten the tape before positioning the artwork.

(Continued)

3 Turn mat and artwork over; press firmly to secure the tape. Secure strip of framer's tape to the mat, directly along the edge of the picture and perpendicular to first strip of tape. Repeat at the opposite end.

4 Cut backing board to the same size as the mat. Position artwork and mat on backing board.

HOW TO HINGE-MOUNT ARTWORK TO A MOUNTING BOARD

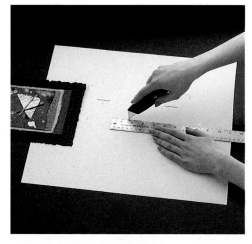

1 Cut mat as desired. Cut mounting board about 2" (5 cm) larger than mat. Determine placement of artwork; using a pencil, lightly mark position at corners, just inside edges of the artwork.

2 Mark two placement lines for hinges on the mounting board as shown, with length of lines ¼" (6 mm) longer than width of framer's tape. Position lines slightly below the markings for upper edge of the artwork and about 1" to 2" (2.5 to 5 cm) from sides. Mark a third line, centered below markings for upper edge, as shown. Using a utility knife and a straightedge, cut a slit at each marking.

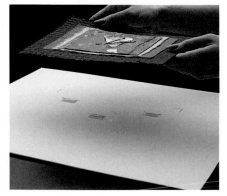

3 Cut three strips of framer's tape about 1½" (3.8 cm) in length. Working from front side of mounting board, insert a strip of tape through each slit, adhesive side up, allowing about ½" (1.3 cm) of tape to extend on front side of board. Secure tape to back side of mounting board.

4 Place artwork, faceup, over front side of mounting board, aligning corners with markings. Press firmly to secure artwork to tape. If using gummed tape, moisten tape before positioning artwork.

5 Place mat over mounting board, with artwork positioned correctly in the opening of mat; mark along the outer edges of mat, using pencil. Cut the mounting board on marked lines. Cut backing board to same size as mounting board.

HOW TO MOUNT ITEMS, USING GLUE

1 Cut mat as desired. Cut mounting board about 2" (5 cm) larger than mat. Determine placement of item; using a pencil, lightly mark position at corners, just inside edges of item.

2 Apply a bead of clear silicone glue or hot glue to back of item; place item over mounting board, aligning edges of item with markings. Allow the silicone glue to cure for 24 hours, or hot glue to cool completely. Complete as in step 5, opposite.

HOW TO MOUNT ITEMS USING HAND STITCHES

1 Cut mat as desired. Cut the mounting board about 2" (5 cm) larger than the mat board. Position the item over mounting board as desired. Determine locations where the item can be supported with small stitches; use a T-pin to mark the mounting board by puncturing it.

2 Remove item. Puncture holes at markings and, again, ⅛" (3 mm) from each marking, using awl.

3 Reposition item. Using thread that matches item, secure it to mounting board at each set of holes, taking about two stitches. From the back of board, tie thread tails, and secure them to board with tape. (Contrasting thread was used to show detail.)

4 Lift mounting board, and check for proper support of item; take additional stitches, if necessary. Complete as in step 5, opposite.

PICTURE & FRAME ASSEMBLY

Picture assembly, called fitting, secures the artwork, mats, glass, and backing or mounting board in the frame. A paper backing, called a dust cover, prevents dust and insects from working their way to the front of the artwork. Rubber bumpers, attached to the lower corners of the frame, allow air to circulate behind the picture and protect the wall.

If necessary, the assembled picture can extend beyond the mounting depth of the frame. Specialty offset hardware is available in several depths to accommodate this type of frame assembly. In general, the boards should not extend more than ¼" (6 mm) beyond the mounting depth of the frame.

When framing valuable artwork, apply an acrylic clear finish to the unfinished wood at the back of the frame before assembling. This sealer protects the artwork from the acids in the wood frame.

For metal sectional frames, follow the manufacturer's directions for assembling and fitting the frame; this style frame generally comes with complete assembly instructions.

Picture-assembly materials and tools, *from top to bottom, include a framer's fitting tool, brown craft paper, foam-core board, artwork, mat, glass, awl, picture wire, rubber bumpers, double-stick transfer tape, frame, screw eyes, brads, and offset hardware.*

HOW TO ASSEMBLE A PICTURE & WOODEN FRAME

MATERIALS

- Wooden picture frame.
- ¾" (2 cm) brads, for attaching frame; or offset hardware and screws.
- Framer's fitting tool or slip-joint pliers, for assembly with brads.
- Brown craft paper and double-stick transfer tape, or ATG tape, for assembly with brads.
- Two screw eyes.
- Self-adhesive rubber bumpers.
- Small awl; picture wire.
- Pressure-sensitive frame-sealing tape, for assembly with offset hardware.

1 Assembly with brads. Cut mat as desired. Mount artwork (pages 39 to 41). Clean both sides of glass thoroughly, using glass cleaner and lint-free cloth. Position glass over picture and mounting board, with edges even; do not slide glass over surface of the mat. Position frame over glass. Check glass for lint or dust. Slide fingers under backing board, and turn frame over.

2 Insert ¾" (2 cm) brads into the middle of each side of the frame, using framer's fitting tool **(a).** Or use slip-joint pliers **(b),** protecting the outside edge of the frame with strip of cardboard.

3 Insert brads along each side, 1" (2.5 cm) from the corners and at about 2" (5 cm) intervals.

4 Attach double-stick transfer tape to back of the frame, about ⅛" (3 mm) from outside edges. Cut brown craft paper 2" (5 cm) larger than the frame; place paper on back of frame, securing it to center of each edge of frame and stretching the paper taut.

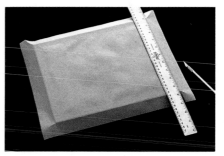

5 Working from center out to each corner, stretch paper and secure to frame. Crease paper over outside edge of frame. Using a straightedge and utility knife, trim the paper about ⅛" (3 mm) inside the creased line.

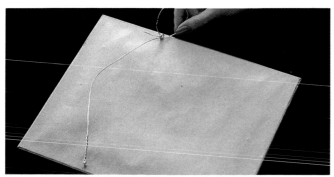

6 Mark placement for the screw eyes, using an awl, about one-third down from the upper edge; secure screw eyes into the frame. Thread wire two or three times through one screw eye; twist the end. Repeat at opposite side, allowing slack; wire is usually about 2" to 3" (5 to 7.5 cm) from top of the frame when hung. Secure rubber bumpers to back of frame, at lower corners.

Assembly with offset hardware. Assemble artwork and frame as in step 1, above; secure in place with offset hardware, spacing hardware about 1½" (3.8 cm) from each corner and at about 6" to 8" (15 to 20.5 cm) intervals; predrill screw holes in hardwood frames. Apply frame-sealing tape to edges of frame to seal assembly. Complete assembly as in step 6.

MULTIPLE MATS

Multiple mats consist of two or more layered mats that have successively larger image openings. These mats provide the opportunity to use several mat colors when framing a single piece of artwork. Multiple mats lead the eye into the image and add depth and richness; the more mats used, the stronger the effect.

Framing shops have mat corner samples available to help you select mat colors. Experiment with different combinations, noticing the features of the artwork that are highlighted with each combination.

A standard width for undermats is ¼" (6 mm); however, this measurement often ranges from ⅛" (3 mm) to ½" (1.3 cm), depending on the look you desire. Different widths can be used in any combination, for a variety of effects. Experiment by layering mat boards in various combinations, exposing different widths for the inner mats to find the arrangement you like best. Keep in mind that light-colored mats will appear wider than dark-colored mats.

When cutting multiple mats, cut the outer, or top, mat first. Then secure the next mat to the back of the completed mat, and cut. Repeat this process for each additional mat.

Precise measuring and cutting are critical when cutting multiple mats. Recheck your calculations to avoid mistakes. Discrepancies of as little as ¹⁄₁₆" (1.5 mm) may be noticeable. For easier reference when cutting, it may be helpful to mark the desired widths for each mat, using a different-colored pencil for each mat.

MATERIALS

- Mat board.
- Basic mat-cutting materials (page 37).
- Double-stick transfer tape, or ATG tape.

HOW TO CUT A MULTIPLE MAT

1 Cut top, or outer, mat board to the outside dimensions as on page 37, step 1. Determine the size of image opening and width of mat borders for bottom, or inner, mat. Mark width of mat borders for bottom mat on top mat, as on page 37, step 2; extend marked lines to edges of mat board.

2 Determine the width of exposed portion of mat border for inner, or first, mat. Mark this measurement on top mat, measuring from previously marked lines toward outside edges of board; extend marked lines to the edges of mat board.

3 Determine the width of exposed portion of second mat. Mark this measurement on top mat as in step 2. Repeat for any additional mats.

4 Cut the image opening in top mat, on outer marked lines as on page 37, steps 3 to 6. Reposition fallout section from top mat for support when cutting. Apply double-stick transfer tape to back side of outer mat along inside edges; apply a short strip of tape to center fallout section.

5 Cut the outside dimensions of mat board for the next mat and any remaining mats ½" (1.3 cm) smaller than top mat. Center next mat facedown, over back side of top mat; press in place.

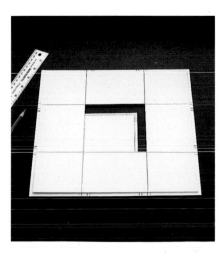

6 Mark width of border for the next mat, using the next set of markings around the edges of the top mat as a guide. Cut mat. Reposition the fallout section and continue as in step 7 if cutting additional mats.

7 Apply double-stick transfer tape to back side of the mat along inside edges and center fallout section. Center next mat facedown over back side of mat; press in place. Continue as in step 6.

MORE IDEAS FOR MULTIPLE MATS

Triple mat with offset corners (below) gives a distinctive look to an old document.

Six mats (bottom, left) in vibrant colors add significance to a child's drawing.

Quadruple mat (left) *draws out colors in the artwork. The mats are cut in a variety of widths for more interest.*

Seven mats (left) *create a mounting depth suitable for framing a dimensional fossil.*

Three monochromatic mats (above) *add richness to a simple display of pressed leaves.*

MATS WITH
MULTIPLE OPENINGS

The Olson Reunion

Display related items in a single mat and frame, using a mat with multiple openings. These mats are perfect for showcasing time-lapse pictures and family photos. Or use a mat with multiple openings to create a space for titling or dating a photograph or piece of artwork.

When cutting mats with multiple openings, treat each opening as a separate, single mat. Completing one opening before starting another ensures that the bevel cuts are at the correct angle.

Because of the precise measurements required, mats with multiple openings are best suited for single mats. It is difficult to cut double or triple mats with multiple openings that align accurately.

Experiment with the positioning of the artwork in order to find a pleasing arrangement. In general, the width of the outer mat border should be the same on all four sides. The width of the mat board between the images is usually narrower than the width of the outer mat border. This helps the images relate to each other and focuses attention inward.

MATERIALS

- Mat board.
- Basic mat-cutting materials (page 37).
- Art eraser.

HOW TO CUT A MAT WITH MULTIPLE OPENINGS

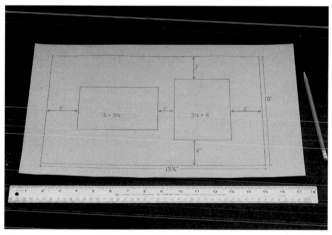

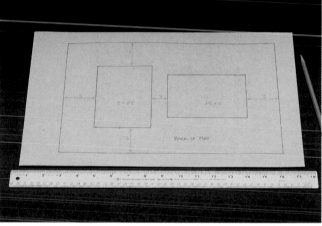

1 Arrange artwork as desired on sheet of paper; determine dimensions of image openings and borders, including outer border. Mark borders and image openings on paper.

2 Transfer markings to back side of paper, if arrangement is not symmetrical. Label for back of mat; use this paper as a guide for marking back of mat board.

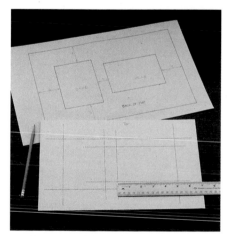

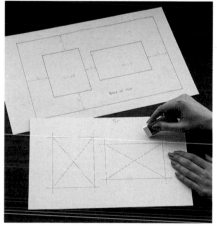

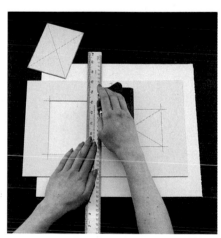

3 Cut mat and mark outer border as on page 37, steps 1 and 2. Transfer the markings for image openings, from paper guide to back of the mat board, extending the marked lines beyond the dimensions of the image openings. Remeasure each opening for accuracy.

4 Mark an X through each image opening. Erase all but ½" (1.3 cm) of lines that are not to be cut, to use as guide for aligning straightedge.

5 Cut image openings as on page 37, steps 3 to 6; complete one opening before starting another.

MORE IDEAS FOR MULTIPLE OPENINGS

Series of rectangular openings creatively highlights artwork.

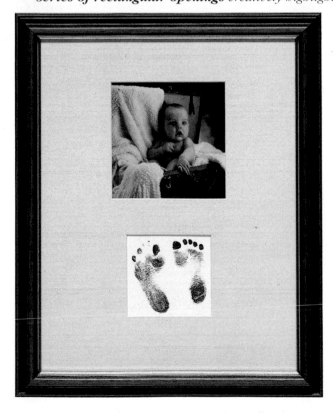

Mask of Courage

Title opening (above) is used to identify a piece of artwork. The angular opening (page 38) follows the contours of the artwork.

Double openings (left) display a baby picture and infant footprints.

Triple openings (opposite) showcase a collection of photos.

RAISED MATS

Create a shadow-box effect for artwork by raising mats above the surface of the mounting board. This technique is used to frame dimensional items, such as handmade paper, jewelry, shells, and coins. Raised mats can also be used with flat artwork to add dimension.

The mats are raised by securing spacer strips of foam-core board, cut slightly narrower than the width of the mat border, to all four sides of the mat. This technique can be applied to all mat styles.

For a basic raised mat, secure spacer strips to the back of a single mat. Spacer strips may be stacked to a depth of about ⅝" (1.5 cm). Layers thicker than this may be visible when the picture is viewed from an angle. This style mat is suitable for framing dimensional objects up to about ½" (1.3 cm) in depth.

For added dimension, separate multiple mats for a stacked-and-layered effect. This technique is quite dramatic and allows deeper framing depths, without the possibility of the foam-core board showing.

Foam-core boards are available in ⅛" and 3⁄16" (3 and 4.5 mm) thicknesses. Choose the board or combination of boards that will give the desired depth for the object you are framing. The glass should not touch the object being framed. If you are stacking foam-core spacers, be sure the mounting depth of the frame can accommodate the thickness of all the layers. It may be necessary to select a shadow-box frame.

Complete all mat cutting and apply any embellishments to the mat (page 56) before securing the spacer strips.

MATERIALS

- Mat board.
- Basic mat-cutting materials (page 37).
- Form-core board.
- Double-stick transfer tape, or ATG tape.

Triple mat (above) is raised between successive mats, adding interest to an architectural print. Single raised mat (opposite) provides the mounting depth needed for displaying a collection of buttons.

HOW TO MAKE A RAISED SINGLE MAT

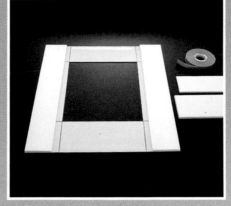
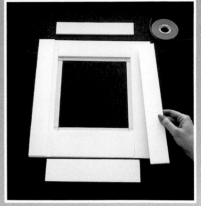

1 Cut single mat (page 37). Mark the dimensions of the spacer strips for sides of mat on foam-core board, with length of strips equal to length of mat sides and width of strips ½" (1.3 cm) narrower than mat border width. Score repeatedly on the marked lines, using a utility knife and straightedge, until the foam-core board is cut through.

2 Cut strips of double-stick transfer tape; secure them to back of the mat board near the outer edges. Position the foam-core strips on sides of mat board, aligning outer edges; press to secure.

3 Cut and apply second layer of spacer strips, if desired, cutting strips ¼" to ½" (6 mm to 1.3 cm) narrower than the previous strips. Repeat, if desired, for third layer.

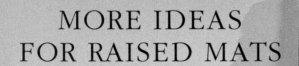

MORE IDEAS FOR RAISED MATS

Raised single mat *gives dimension to pressed leaves and handmade paper.*

Raised mat with window-pane opening *gives the effect of looking out through a window. Inner panels are supported with narrow strips of foam-core board.*

HOW TO MAKE A RAISED MULTIPLE MAT

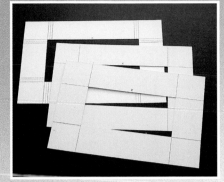

1 Cut multiple mat (page 45); in step 4, use short strips of double-stick transfer tape positioned toward outer edges of the mat. Gently separate mats; center and mark an X along inner opening of same side of each mat to use as guides for realignment.

2 Cut and secure spacer strips to back of top mat, following steps 1 and 2, opposite. Secure strips of double-stick transfer tape to back of spacer strips.

3 Center top mat faceup, over face side of inner mat, aligning marked sides; press in place. Repeat for each successive mat.

Raised mat with multiple openings *displays flat artwork and dimensional floral materials.*

Mount flat artwork (page 39), and support with separate backing board. Secure backing board to mat board, using double-stick transfer tape; then apply foam-core spacer strips to mat as in steps 1 and 2, opposite.

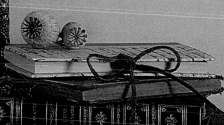

EMBELLISHED MATS

Mats can be embellished using ink lines, strips of graphic tape or marbleized paper, and decorative rub-on transfers. Each method has its own distinctive style. The methods can also be combined for additional interest.

Embellished mats are usually used when a traditional look is desired; however, contemporary effects can also be achieved.

Decorating mats with ink lines, often referred to as French lines, was originally done using French line pens and inkwells. The same effects are easily achieved using permanent, fine-point markers.

Pressure-sensitive tape gives the effect of French lines with a slightly bolder look. This tape is available in several widths and colors at stationery and office supply stores.

French lines are generally marked close to the inner edge of the mat to draw the eye inward. Multiple lines are usually spaced no more than ½" (1.3 cm) apart. In general, use light-colored lines near the inner edge of the mat and dark lines near the outer edge.

For a more vibrant accent, apply narrow strips of marbleized paper around the image opening. These strips are usually applied as single bands, generally ranging in width from ⅛" to ⅜" (3 mm to 1 cm). Bands wider than this detract from the artwork. Framing shops supply self-adhesive pieces of marbleized paper in a variety of colors. Or make your own strips, using marbleized paper and double-stick transfer tape. When selecting papers, choose one with a dominant color that is repeated in the artwork.

Rub-on transfers, designed especially for embellishing mats, are available in a variety of designs, including flourishes, lines, and letters. For best results, keep the applications simple. One or two flourishes are usually all that is needed.

Choose smooth-surfaced mats and complete all cutting before applying embellishments. These techniques are not suitable for heavily textured or fabric mats. Avoid metallic mats when using ink lines. You may want to test the technique first on a scrap piece of the mat board. When applying multiple rows, start at the inner edges of the mat and work toward the outer edges.

HOW TO EMBELLISH A MAT
USING INK LINES

MATERIALS

- Mat.
- Permanent, fine-point markers.
- Metal straightedge.
- Art eraser.

1 Mark placement of lines on right side of mat, with short marks at outer edges of mat. Mark start and stop of each line with a light pencil line ¼" to ½" (6 mm to 1.3 cm) long.

2 Align a straightedge so the markings are just visible. Holding marker in an upright position, mark line on one side of the mat, using one continuous motion; start and stop the line just inside markings. Lift marker.

(Continued)

3 Turn mat 180° to opposite side; align straightedge, and mark the line. Allow ink lines to dry; then mark lines on remaining sides. Repeat to draw any additional lines. Allow ink to dry.

4 Erase pencil marks, using an art eraser and a light, circular motion.

HOW TO EMBELLISH A MAT USING PRESSURE-SENSITIVE TAPE

MATERIALS

- Mat.
- Pressure-sensitive tape.
- Metal straightedge.
- Mat knife.
- Artist's burnisher; tracing paper.
- Art eraser.

1 Follow page 57, step 1. Cut tape about 2" (5 cm) longer than needed. Holding tape taut, align with marked line; lightly smooth in place, leaving excess tape at ends loose. Repeat on opposite side.

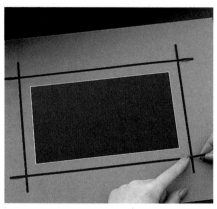

2 Apply tape to the remaining sides, overlapping ends at corners.

3 Position straightedge diagonally over corner of mat at 45° angle to tape. Using mat knife, cut through the upper strip of tape. Remove the trimmed end.

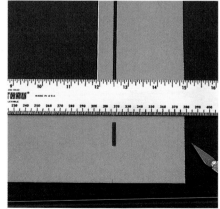

4 Trim the remaining excess tape even with outer edge of tape on adjacent side, using straightedge and mat knife.

5 Repeat steps 3 and 4 at remaining corners. Place tracing paper over tape; rub gently, using burnisher and taking care not to mar mat. Erase any pencil marks, using art eraser and light, circular motion.

HOW TO EMBELLISH A MAT USING MARBLEIZED PAPER

MATERIALS

- Mat.
- Marbleized paper.
- Double-stick transfer tape or ATG tape.
- Hard-lead, sharp pencil.
- Mat knife.
- Metal straightedge.
- Artist's burnisher; tracing paper.

1 Cut a piece of marbleized paper about 4" (10 cm) longer than desired length of the strips. Apply double-stick transfer tape to back of paper, butting the edges; do not remove backing strip from the tape.

2 Mark right side of the paper along short ends for the desired width and number of strips. Align straightedge with marks for first strip. Using a mat knife with sharp blade, lightly score paper; repeat two or three times to cut through the paper. Gradual cutting helps seal the raw, white edges of the paper. Repeat to cut desired number of strips.

3 Mark the mat and apply paper strips as for pressure-sensitive tape, steps 1 to 5, opposite; remove paper backing from strips.

HOW TO EMBELLISH MATS USING RUB-ON TRANSFERS

MATERIALS

- Mat.
- Rub-on transfers.
- Artist's burnisher; tracing paper.

1 Remove the backing paper from transfer sheet; position the design as desired on the mat surface. Using burnisher, gently rub over design; design will lighten in color as it is released.

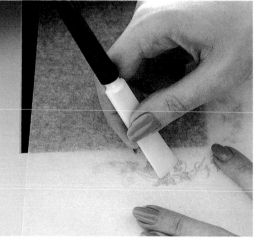

2 Lift the transfer sheet. Place backing sheet over the design; rub over design, using a burnisher.

MORE IDEAS FOR EMBELLISHED MATS

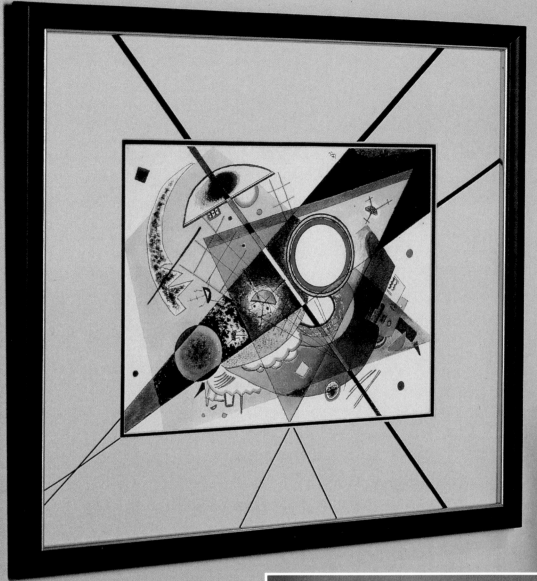

Pressure-sensitive tape *(above) is used to extend the design lines in the artwork onto the mat for added drama.*

Strips of paper *embellish a double mat with colors found in the print.*

Spattered paint (above) accents a handmade paper collage. Combine two parts paint with one part water; spatter the paint over the mat by striking the paintbrush against a paint stick.

Stamped paw-print design adds a whimsical touch to an animal print.

FRAMING NEEDLE ARTS

Needle art, including cross-stitch, crewelwork, drawnwork, and needlepoint, adds a warm, personal touch to wall displays. Framing and matting draw attention to the piece and offer protection.

In order to display needle art without any wrinkles or bubbles, stretch fabric or canvas artwork around a foam-core mounting board. When mounting needlepoint, which requires firmer stretching, reinforce the foam-core board with a piece of mat board.

Needle-art pieces worked on fabric can be secured to the mounting board using double-stick transfer tape or sequin pins. The tape method is quick and easy; however, the tape may discolor the fabric over time. For needle-art pieces of value, sequin pins are recommended; the pins can be removed if you decide you want to use the piece for another project at a later date. Because of the firmer stretching required for needlepoint projects, the canvas is stapled to the mounting board.

For easy mounting, allow several inches of fabric or canvas on each side of the design. If necessary, fabric strips can be stitched to the sides of the needle-art design. Be sure the needle art is clean before stretching it. Needlepoint pieces may need to be blocked before framing. Clip any loose threads on the back side, since loose thread tails may create streaks on the finished piece.

In order to accurately position the needle-art design in the image opening of the mat, the mounting board is cut smaller than the frame opening. This allows you to adjust the position of the mounting board, if the needle art is not accurately centered.

A single mat is often all that is needed to raise the glass above the surface of the stitching. If additional space is needed between the glass and the stitching, cut a multiple mat (page 44) or raised mat (page 53). For the best protection of all needle-art projects, use acid-free foam-core boards and mat boards.

MATERIALS

- 3⁄16" (4.5 mm) foam-core board.
- Mat board and packing tape, for stretching needlepoint.
- Stainless steel T-pins.
- Double-stick transfer tape or ATG tape; framer's tape.
- Sequin pins, for stretching needle art worked on fabric, optional.
- Heavy-duty stapler and 3⁄16" (4.5 mm) staples, for stretching needlepoint.
- Utility knife and straightedge.
- Firmly woven fabric, if necessary to increase size of needle art.

HOW TO STRETCH NEEDLE ART WORKED ON FABRIC

1 **Double-stick transfer tape.** Cut foam-core board at least 2" (5 cm) larger than the image opening of mat.

2 Stitch strips of firmly woven fabric to sides of the needle art, if necessary to increase size; allow at least 1" (2.5 cm) on each side for wrapping and stretching fabric around board.

(Continued)

3 Center the needle art, right side up, over foam-core board. Insert a T-pin, through fabric and into the edge of foam-core, at center of one side. Aligning grain of fabric with edge of board, pin fabric at each corner of same side, pulling the fabric taut between pins. Repeat to stretch and pin fabric to adjacent side, then remaining sides.

4 Stretch and pin the fabric between the T-pins, completing one side at a time and spacing T-pins about every ½" (1.3 cm).

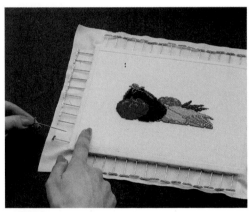

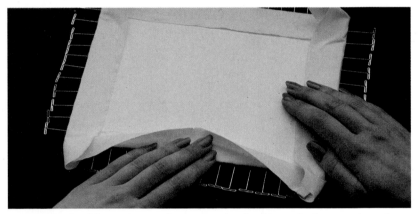

5 Recheck that design is straight; repin as necessary. Check that the fabric is taut by smoothing finger across piece; you should not be able to push any excess fabric. Repin fabric as necessary.

6 Secure double-stick transfer tape to back of board, close to the edges; apply second layer of tape over the previous layer. Wrap excess fabric to back of board, pulling firmly and securing to tape; complete one side at a time, starting in the center and working toward corners.

7 Remove T-pins. Fold fabric at the corners, trimming any excess; secure with tape. Secure needle art to mat board (opposite).

Sequin pins.
Follow pages 63 and 64, steps 1 to 5. Insert sequin pins into edges of the board, at ¼" (6 mm) intervals, removing T-pins. Fold in the excess fabric at corners; secure with hand stitching. Secure needle art to mat board (opposite).

HOW TO STRETCH NEEDLEPOINT

1 Cut the foam-core board 1" to 2" (2.5 to 5 cm) larger than the image opening of the mat. Cut a piece of mat board the same size as the foam-core board; secure to the foam-core board, using double-stick transfer tape. Mat board side is the back of the mounting board.

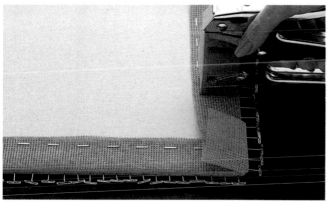

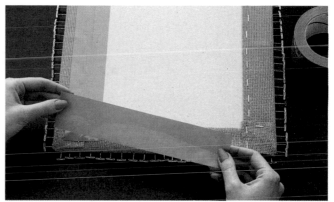

2 Stretch and secure needlepoint following steps 3 to 5 opposite. Wrap the excess canvas to back side of the board, pulling firmly, and staple. Complete one side at a time, starting in center and working toward corners. Fold in excess canvas at corners; staple.

3 Secure raw edges of canvas to back of the board, using packing tape. Remove T-pins. Secure needle art to mat board (below).

HOW TO SECURE STRETCHED NEEDLE ART
TO A MAT BOARD

1 Position mat over needle art, centering design. Holding needle art and mat firmly, turn piece over; tape needle art to mat board, using framer's tape.

2 Cut pieces of foam-core board to fill the areas between needle art and edge of the mat board; secure each piece to the mat, using double-stick transfer tape. Cut the backing board to same size as the top mat. Assemble the picture (page 42).

Creative
Framing
Ideas

PAPER-COVERED FRAMES

Give a new look to an old frame by covering it with decorative paper. Add other embellishments as desired, such as decorative tacks or paper cutouts.

Art supply stores carry papers in a variety of textures and colors, including corrugated paper and papers with grasses and fiber strands embedded in them. For best results, choose medium to heavyweight papers, because the tape that secures the paper to the frame may show through translucent papers. To protect the paper, display the frames away from direct sunlight.

HOW TO COVER A FRAME WITH PAPER

MATERIALS

- Picture frame with flat surface.
  - Decorative paper.
  - Double-stick transfer tape, or ATG tape.
  - Paint, for inside edges of frame; optional.
  - Decorative tacks, drill and $\frac{1}{16}$" drill bit, optional.

1 Paint the inside edges of the frame opening, if desired; inside edges are covered with paper. Place the frame facedown over wrong side of paper; mark along the outer edges and the inner opening of frame. Measure the thickness of the frame. Mark lines on paper, adding this measurement to outer marked lines.

2 Cut along inner and outer marked lines, using a straightedge and a utility knife or a rotary cutter; for heavy papers, cut slightly outside the marked lines to allow for fold. Extend inner lines to outer lines at the corners; cut out corner squares as shown. Apply double-stick transfer tape to face of frame along inner and outer edges.

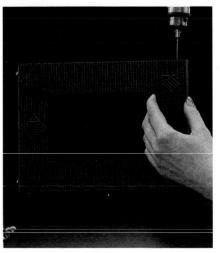

3 Center the frame over the back side of paper: press in place. Score heavy papers with a dull table knife along outer edges of frame. Apply double-stick transfer tape to sides of frame; wrap paper over the sides, and press paper in place.

4 Apply embellishments, if desired, securing with glue or tacks; if using tacks, predrill the holes, using a $\frac{1}{16}$" drill bit, to prevent splitting hardwood frames.

Give a whimsical look to a plain frame by applying simple motifs cut from copper or tin. Embellish the motifs to produce a variety of textures, including embossed, oxidized, and brushed. Nails, decorative tacks, or glue can be used to secure the metal accents to the frame.

Small copper and tin sheets and metal foils for embossing are available at craft stores and mail order suppliers. Copper is the thinner of the two metals, and it can be cut easily with household utility scissors. Tin can be cut best with jeweler's snips, available at jewelry-making supply stores.

HOW TO EMBELLISH A FRAME WITH METAL ACCENTS

MATERIALS

- Wooden frame.
- Copper or tin sheets, or 36-gauge metal foil, for embossed design.
- Utility scissors or jeweler's snips.
- Transfer paper, optional, for transferring embossing design.
- Scrap of wood.
- 100-grit sandpaper; 0000 steel wool.
- Tongs with handles that do not conduct heat, for oxidizing copper.
- 60-grit sandpaper, for brushed metal.
- Hammer and scrap of corrugated cardboard, for hammered effect.
- Patina solution, for antique verdigris finish on copper.
- Glue, or nails or decorative tacks.
- Aerosol clear acrylic sealer.

1 Mark outline of metal accent on metal sheet or foil. Embellish the metal foil with an embossed design, if desired (opposite).

2 Cut on the marked lines, using scissors or jeweler's snips. Trim tips off any sharp points.

3 Place metal accents right side up over a scrap of wood. Using an awl, punch holes where nails or tacks will be used to secure the accents to the frame.

4 Sand edges of metal accents, using sandpaper to smooth any sharp edges of metal; avoid sanding surface of design if smooth finish is desired. Buff surface of metal, using steel wool. Embellish the metal accents with an oxidized, brushed, hammered, or antiqued finish as desired (opposite).

5 Apply several light coats of aerosol clear acrylic sealer to metal accents. Secure the metal accents to the frame, using nails, tacks, or glue. Predrill holes, using drill bit slightly smaller than nails or tacks.

TIPS FOR EMBELLISHING METAL

Embossed. Place metal foil on several layers of newspaper. Draw or trace the desired embossing design on paper. For an asymmetrical design, reverse the design. Tape the embossing design to the metal sheet. Using a pen with a ball point, trace along the design lines; retrace lines as necessary for desired detail.

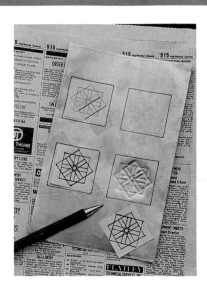

Oxidized copper. Hold copper accent over flame, using tongs. Remove from heat and check color occasionally; holding copper in flame too long causes copper to lose all of its natural color.

Hammered effect. Place copper or tin accent on a piece of corrugated cardboard, and cover with sheet of paper. Using a hammer, pound the copper for desired effect. Repeat on the back side.

Brushed surface. Texturize copper or tin by sanding metal lightly.

Verdigris finish. Apply chemical solution for reproducing antique verdigris finish to copper, following manufacturer's directions.

MARBLEIZED FRAMES

The subtle and elegant colors of these marbleized frames are easy to produce using aerosol enamel paints. Paint is floated in water; then the frame is dipped into the water to pick up the color randomly. The process can be repeated with multiple colors to produce a frame with a mottled, textural effect.

This technique can be used on flat-surfaced or dimensional frames. Since no two marbleized frames are alike, this technique is especially attractive for frames that are grouped together.

HOW TO ADD DECORATIVE BUNDLES TO A FRAME

MATERIALS

- Wooden picture frame.
- 24-gauge or 28-gauge copper or brass craft wire.
- Natural materials as desired for bundles.
- Drill and 1/16" drill bit.

1 Assemble bundles. Wrap each bundle several times with wire; twist wire on the back side, leaving about 4" (10 cm) excess wire at ends for securing bundle to frame.

2 Arrange the bundles as desired on the frame; using a pencil, mark the location for the holes, marking two dots about 1/4" (6 mm) apart for each bundle. Drill holes at the marked dots, using a 1/16" drill bit.

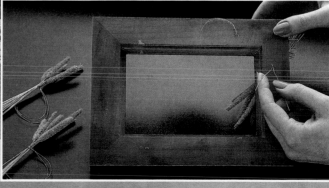

3 Insert the wire ends of bundle through holes; twist ends tightly behind the frame to secure bundle. Repeat for the remaining bundles. Trim excess wire.

MORE IDEAS FOR CREATIVE FRAMING

Curly willow *adds drama and texture to a framed mirror. The curly willow is secured with 16-gauge wire nails; to prevent splitting the wood, predrill the holes, using a 1/16" drill bit. Copper charms are wired to the twigs for interest.*

Wired ribbon bow, *trimmed with a brass charm, embellishes the top of a traditional frame. Secure the bow and charm to the frame with hot glue.*

Painted wooden medallion, *secured with glue, adds a raised design to a simple frame. Before attaching the medallion, give the frame a marbleized finish as on page 75.*

Multicolored painted frame
enhances artwork. Paint the frame
in sections, masking off areas as
necessary, using tape.

Beads, secured to the edges of a frame with nails,
provide a colorful accent. Holes are predrilled into
the edges of the frame; then 16-gauge nails, threaded
with beads, are inserted into the holes and secured
in place with a dot of glue.

Brass knobs (right) serve as key hooks on a wide,
wooden frame. Predrill the holes for the knobs.

Stones and glass gems (below), selected
to complement the artwork, are secured to
a painted frame with hot glue.

DISPLAYING ARTWORK ON CANVASES

Artist's canvases provide a quick and inexpensive way to display artwork such as photographs, postcards, and greeting cards. The white canvas serves as a mat. Pine lath, nailed around the edges of the canvas, becomes the frame.

Prestretched cotton canvases, stapled to a wooden frame, are available at art supply stores and craft stores and come in many sizes. Select the dimensions that will give the desired border width around the artwork.

The artwork is secured to the canvas with double-stick transfer tape, or ATG tape. For this reason, and because the artwork is not protected by glass, this mounting and display method is not recommended for artwork that is valuable.

MATERIALS

- Artist's prestretched cotton canvas.
- $\frac{1}{4}$" × $1\frac{3}{8}$" (6 mm × 3.5 cm) pine lath.
- Paint, or stain and matching putty, for pine lath.
- 16 × $\frac{3}{4}$" (2 cm) brads; nail set.
- Drill and $\frac{1}{16}$" drill bit.
- Double-stick transfer tape or ATG tape.
- Rubber bumpers; sawtooth picture hanger.

HOW TO DISPLAY ARTWORK USING AN ARTIST'S CANVAS

1 Cut pine lath to length of canvas top and bottom. Repeat for sides, adding $\frac{1}{2}$" (1.3 cm) to length of side lath strips to allow for overlap of lath at ends. Sand ends lightly; apply a paint or stain to lath strips.

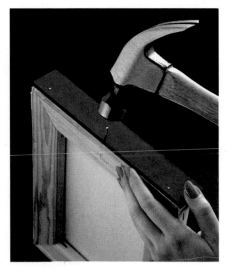

2 Align the top lath strip to wooden frame of stretched canvas, at the back edge and ends of frame. Secure with brads; predrill holes, and space the brads about 1" (2.5 cm) from the ends and at about 5" (12.5 cm) intervals. Repeat to secure bottom lath strip; then secure the side strips.

3 Secure each corner with a brad, predrilling holes. Countersink brads, using a nail set; fill holes with putty to match stain, or touch up with paint.

4 Apply double-stick transfer tape to back side of artwork along the outer edges; for larger pieces, apply one or more additional strips in the center area. Position artwork as desired on the canvas; press in place. Secure the sawtooth hanger to back of frame, centering at the upper edge. Secure rubber bumpers at lower corners.

MORE IDEAS FOR DISPLAYING ARTWORK

Empty frame, *propped against the wall, provides an opportunity to showcase three-dimensional star and moon forms. The framed objects are suspended from the frame with monofilament fishing line. The remaining items are secured to the wall with silicone glue.*

Weathered board *is the mounting surface for this nature picture. Narrow strips of leather, secured to the board with tacks, hold the image in place.*

Clipboards *(right), hung on the wall, allow children's artwork to be changed with ease. The clipboards are personalized with paint pens.*

Foam-core board is used as a background for dry-mounted prints. Dry-mounting is done professionally at custom framing shops.

Double layer of glass replaces the traditional frame assembly, allowing the wall to become the mat. This interesting technique, however, does not protect the artwork indefinitely.

DECORATIVE HANGING METHODS

Decorative hangers are used as nonfunctional accessories to provide interest to walls and artwork. Often used to link pictures together, decorative hangers can also be used to highlight a color, add texture, or visually increase the size of a wall grouping.

Cording adds elegance to traditional pictures. Accentuate the look, if desired, with tassels. For an old-world look, mount the cording high on the wall or at the ceiling level.

For a tailored accent, hang a picture using an ornate ring pull. Ring pulls are available in a variety of sizes and finishes at craft stores, hardware stores, and specialty woodworking stores. Hang the ring pulls from small nails or decorative hangers.

Decorative drawer pulls and ribbon can add a clean, tailored accent or a vintage look to a display, depending on the style of hardware and ribbon chosen. Select drawer pulls with wood thread screws, suitable for mounting to the wall. Other knobs intended for use with a bolt may be converted for use as decorative hangers by substituting a hanger bolt for the original bolt.

HOW TO HANG A PICTURE WITH CORDING

MATERIALS

- Cording; tassels, optional.
- Brad.
- Transparent or masking tape.

1 Hang picture (page 30). Fold the cording in half, and tie overhand knot about 2" (5 cm) from fold. Hand-stitch one or two tassels to knot, if desired. Secure the cording to the wall as desired, using brad; conceal the brad in knot.

2 Determine the desired drape of cording; pin-mark length at upper edge of frame. Remove cording from wall. Wrap tape around the cording about ½" (1.3 cm) below the pin marks; trim cording. Secure the cording to back of the frame with tape. Rehang the picture.

Drawer pulls and grosgrain ribbon
unite a trio of nature prints.

Ring pull and decorative hanger
add interest to a traditional print.

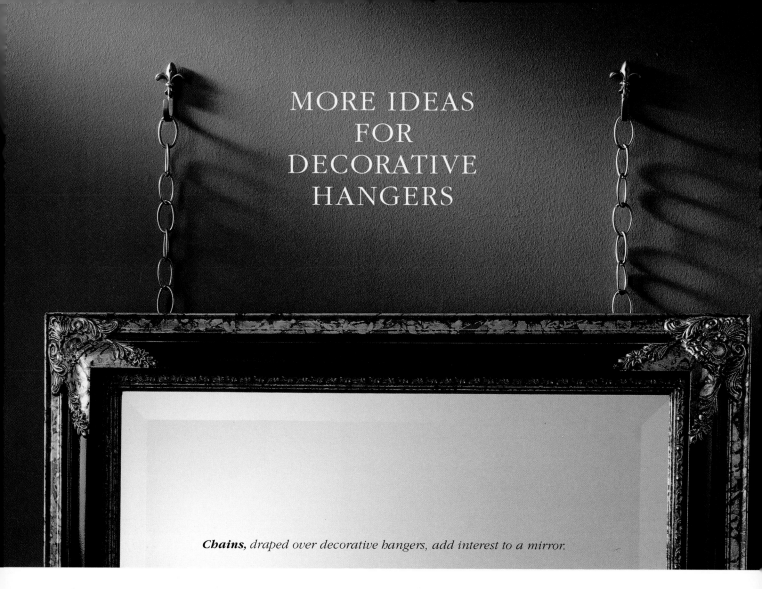

MORE IDEAS
FOR
DECORATIVE
HANGERS

Chains, draped over decorative hangers, add interest to a mirror.

HOW TO HANG A PICTURE WITH A DRAWER PULL & RIBBON

MATERIALS

- Decorative drawer pull.
- Ribbon.
- Hanger bolt, if necessary, for securing drawer pull to wall.
- Drill and drill bit.
- Utility tape.

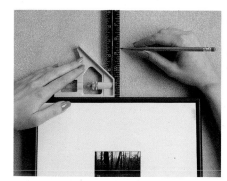

1 Hang the picture (page 30). Mark position on wall for drawer pull, taking care to center the mark above picture. Attach hanger bolt to drawer pull, if necessary. Secure drawer pull to wall; predrill hole, using drill bit slightly smaller than screw.

2 Drape the ribbon over the drawer pull. Pin-mark the length of ribbon at upper edge of frame, keeping the ribbon taut.

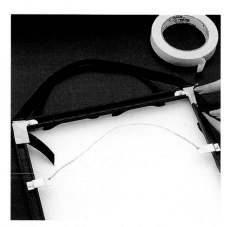

3 Secure ribbon to back of frame with tape, aligning pin marks to upper edge of frame. Rehang picture.

Ribbon, ring pull, and drawer pull are combined to add height and prominence to a picture.

Plaster relief is paired with a tapestry ribbon to create a decorative hanger.

HOW TO HANG A PICTURE WITH A RING PULL

MATERIALS

- Decorative ring pull.
- Decorative hanger or brass nail.
- Awl.
- Drill and drill bit.

1 Mark the center of frame at upper edge, using awl. Predrill hole, using drill bit slightly smaller than the ring pull screw.

2 Secure the ring pull to the frame. Hang the picture (page 30). Mark location for nail or decorative hanger, and tap into position.

Floral
Accessories

FLORAL-EMBELLISHED MIRROR FRAMES

Enhance an inexpensive or secondhand mirror with floral accents. For a dramatic look, cover a large portion of the frame with moss and floral materials. Or, for a more subtle look, embellish one or two corners of the frame. Both styles can be made using either sheet moss or foliage for the base. Dried, silk, or parchment floral materials add color.

To help preserve an arrangement from dried floral materials, apply a matte aerosol acrylic finish and avoid displaying the mirror where it will receive direct sunlight. For longer-lasting displays, select silk or parchment floral materials.

Floral materials *add a touch of romance to framed mirrors. Use the floral materials as accents in the corners, allowing a portion of the frame to remain visible, or use them to cover the entire frame (inset).*

MATERIALS

- Framed mirror.
- Sheet moss, or dried or silk foliage, for base.
- Floral materials as desired.
- Hot glue gun and glue sticks.
- Aerosol clear acrylic sealer, for arrangement from dried floral materials.

HOW TO MAKE A FLORAL-EMBELLISHED MIRROR FRAME

1 **Sheet moss base.** Cover desired areas of the frame with sheet moss, securing it with hot glue. Mist the moss lightly, to make it more pliable.

2 Secure embellishments to frame as desired, using hot glue; apply items one variety at a time, working from largest item to smallest item.

3 Cover mirror, using newspaper and masking tape. Apply aerosol clear acrylic sealer to dried floral arrangements, to help preserve them.

Foliage base. Arrange foliage on the frame to form a base for the flowers; secure with hot glue. Complete the arrangement as in steps 2 and 3.

SEASONAL MANTELS

Mantels and fireplaces are ideal places for adding seasonal changes to your decorating. Arrangements can be changed easily without adding nail holes to walls, and since this area is often the focal point of a room, any changes have high impact.

Autumn arrangement (opposite) features a garland of twigs, preserved leaves, and bittersweet, draped over the mantel.

Make the garland by wiring clusters of twigs and leaves to a rope base. Secure the sprigs of bittersweet with hot glue.

Spring arrangement includes a collection of pots filled with silk tulips, crocuses, hyancinths, and Spanish moss. For interest, the height of the pots is varied. Wreath embellished with found objects (page 98) is hung above the mantel.

Summer arrangement of tiered flowers fills the fireplace. A framed landscape and pots of silk foliage complete the look. The arrangement is simply made by inserting floral foam into a terra-cotta container, then inserting floral materials in rows, for a tiered display.

Winter arrangement with an evergreen garland base has clustered parchment flowers at the center. The arrangement is accented with pinecones, ornaments, and artificial-snow-covered sprigs of greenery.

SEASONAL WALL BASKETS

Wall baskets with floral arrangements add interest to walls. Change the look throughout the year by selecting flowers that reflect the seasons. For long-lasting arrangements, select silk or parchment floral materials.

For arrangements with soft, subtle colors, use dried floral materials. A wide variety of silk, preserved, and dried floral materials is available at floral shops and craft stores.

For easy arrangements, choose two or three foliage materials to form a base for the flowers. Then choose flowers, in several sizes, that are appropriate for the season. Accent the arrangement, if desired, with items such as pinecones, pomegranates, ribbon or raffia bows, and small twigs.

Summer basket (opposite) *displays several varieties of colorful floral materials.*

Spring basket (above) *features clustered lilacs and daffodils inserted into a base of ivy. Pussy willow stems, plumosa, and freesia are added for more texture.*

Fall basket *consists of several preserved foliage materials, accented with dried hydrangea and artichokes. Poppy pods, bittersweet, and curly willow stems provide additional interest.*

Winter basket *has a base of preserved juniper. Berry stems, dried pepper stems, pinecones, and pomegranates add visual interest. Curly willow stems are sprayed gold for a festive look.*

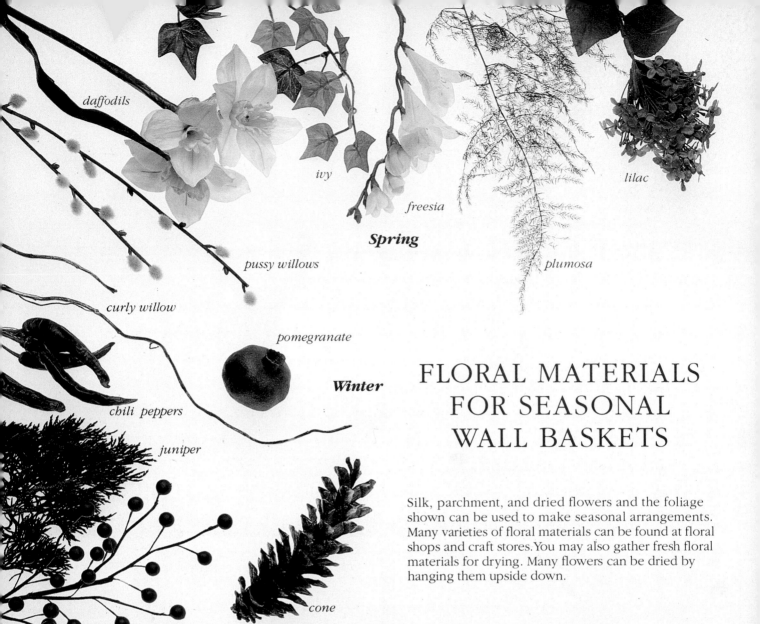

daffodils

ivy

freesia

lilac

Spring

pussy willows

plumosa

curly willow

pomegranate

Winter

FLORAL MATERIALS FOR SEASONAL WALL BASKETS

chili peppers

juniper

Silk, parchment, and dried flowers and the foliage shown can be used to make seasonal arrangements. Many varieties of floral materials can be found at floral shops and craft stores. You may also gather fresh floral materials for drying. Many flowers can be dried by hanging them upside down.

cone

berries

HOW TO MAKE A SEASONAL WALL BASKET

MATERIALS

- Wall basket.
- Floral foam for silk or dried arranging; serrated knife; brown craft paper.
- Sheet moss or Spanish moss.
- Silk, parchment, or dried foliage in one or more varieties.
- Silk, parchment, or dried flowers in various sizes.
- Embellishments, optional.
- Hot glue gun and glue sticks.
- Aerosol clear acrylic sealer, for dried arrangements.

1 Line interior of basket with crumpled paper, to cover any open areas of basket. Using the knife, cut foam to fit the basket, allowing ease; extend the foam about 2" (5 cm) above the basket. Cover foam with moss.

2 Insert first variety of foliage into the container; place the taller stems into the center near the back and the shorter stems at the sides and front, fanning the materials out evenly. Insert any remaining varieties of foliage or small filler flowers, one variety at a time, spacing them evenly.

sweet peas

asters

astilbe

irises

cosmos

Summer

Fall

oak leaves

bittersweet

artichoke

seeded eucalyptus

hydrangea

twigs

poppy pods

3 Insert any large flowers into arrangement, one variety at a time, spacing them evenly throughout to keep the arrangement balanced on three sides.

4 Insert any medium-size flowers into the arrangement to fill in any bare areas. Insert embellishments as desired, securing with hot glue. Apply aerosol clear acrylic sealer to dried floral arrangements.

WREATHS EMBELLISHED WITH FOUND OBJECTS

A wreath is a traditional wall accent that can complement many decorating styles. For a wreath with a dynamic effect, make the focal point of the wreath a found object, such as a vintage container, teapot, or musical instrument.

For a wreath with a loose, airy design and a woodsy look, use a large coil of honeysuckle vine. Honeysuckle coils are available at many floral shops and craft stores. A similar loose, airy effect can be achieved by loosely wrapping a grapevine wreath with a second wreath that has been uncoiled.

Wreath (left), from grapevine, is embellished with a birdhouse, a craft bird's nest, and floral materials. Wreath made from honeysuckle coil (above) has a vintage instrument for the focal point. Floral materials and ribbon add color to the wreath.

HOW TO MAKE A WREATH EMBELLISHED WITH A FOUND OBJECT

MATERIALS

- Honeysuckle vine coil or two grapevine wreaths of the same size.
- Found object, for focal point.
- Dried seeded eucalyptus, boxwood, and magnolia, or three other varieties of dried or silk foliage.
- Dried or silk dominant floral materials, such as hydrangea and sorghum.
- Dried or silk filler materials, such as pepper berries and chili peppers.
- Embellishments, such as ribbons or pomegranates.
- 22-gauge or 24-gauge paddle floral wire; wire cutter; hot glue gun and glue sticks.
- Aerosol clear acrylic sealer, for dried arrangements.

1 Honeysuckle coil. Secure the found object carefully to the wreath, using wire. Tie ribbon or raffia around item, if desired, to conceal wire.

2 Insert the foliage into wreath, one variety at a time, securing with hot glue; concentrate foliage near found object. Apply hot glue to dominant floral materials; secure to the wreath.

3 Insert filler materials into wreath, to fill in any bare areas; insert items one variety at a time, securing them with hot glue.

4 Secure any embellishments with hot glue. Apply aerosol clear acrylic sealer to the dried arrangements; protect found object with plastic wrap, if desired. Make a wire loop for hanging the wreath; secure around a cluster of vines at back of wreath.

Grapevine wreaths. Loosen coils of one wreath; position over the remaining wreath, and arrange vines for a loose, airy effect. Attach vines to the lower wreath, using floral wire. Continue as in steps 1 to 4, above.

Birdcages, mounted on a wall or suspended from a wall bracket, soften the decor in a room and add an airy, dimensional element. For added impact, embellish the top and base of the birdcage to create a wall accent that is decorative from all angles.

When working on the arrangement, hang the cage at the level at which it will be displayed. Stand back several times as you are applying the embellishments to check the placement of the floral materials. If the arrangement will be viewed from a seated postion, evaluate the design from below.

MATERIALS

- Birdcage.
- Sheet moss.
- Twigs or branches, such as birch or curly willow.
- Dried or silk dominant flowers, such as hydrangea.
- Dried or silk filler materials, such as roses,

pepper berries, statice, Queen Anne's lace, and sprigs of greenery.
- Ribbon.
- Floral tape; hot glue gun and glue sticks.
- Aerosol clear acrylic sealer, for dried arrangements.

Wall-mounted birdcage (above) is embellished with variegated ivy, fruit, and flowers. Wire birdcage (opposite) has dried floral materials secured to the top and bottom of the cage.

HOW TO EMBELLISH A BIRDCAGE

1 Secure sheet moss to top of birdcage, using hot glue; extend moss randomly over sides. Repeat for the bottom of cage. Mist the sheet moss lightly before securing, if desired, to make it more pliable.

2 Apply twigs to top and bottom of birdcage, securing them with hot glue.

3 Secure multiple stems of filler materials together with floral tape; secure to the birdcage with hot glue.

4 Tuck additional filler materials in bare areas, securing with hot glue. Apply an aerosol clear acrylic sealer to dried arrangements.

5 Drape ribbon on top of birdcage, allowing ribbon to cascade over the edge in soft folds; secure with glue in several places.

DICKINSON AREA PUBLIC LIBRARY

SWAGS

This vertical floral swag is both pretty and practical. Hung alone, it gracefully fills a narrow wall space. Displayed on both sides of a picture or mirror, a pair of swags can add significance to a display.

The base of the swag, made using twigs, can be constructed in many sizes. Determine the desired length and width of the twig base; then choose flowers that are appropriate for the size of the base. For proper balance, larger bases will require larger focal flowers. When making pairs of swags, insert the flowers for symmetrical arrangements.

HOW TO MAKE A SWAG

MATERIALS

- Twigs, such as birch or dogwood.
- Silk, parchment, or dried flowers in three sizes.
- Barley or other grain material.

- Grape clusters or berry stems.
- Foliage materials, such as leaves, ferns, or ivy.

- 20-gauge or 22-gauge paddle floral wire; wire cutter.
- Hot glue gun and glue sticks.

1 Cut and bundle twigs to desired finished length of swag, with tips of twigs at both ends. Wrap tightly with wire to secure. Repeat for desired finished width. Place short bundle on long bundle about one-third down from top; secure with wire. Reserve several twigs for use in step 6.

2 Insert largest flower into twig base to one side of center as shown; trim stem as necessary. Secure with hot glue.

3 Insert the remaining large flowers into the arrangement, then smaller flowers, placing flowers for a staggered vertical arrangement. Secure with hot glue.

4 Trim barley to about 7" (18 cm) in length. Cluster several stems together; secure with wire. Glue the clusters into arrangement to fill in any bare areas.

5 Insert grape clusters or berry stems, arranging them to cascade outward and downward; secure with hot glue.

6 Insert foliage materials, one variety at a time, to soften and fill out the swag. Glue additional twigs as desired for dimension and to round out shape of base. Secure wire loop for hanging to back side of swag.

WALL BUNDLES

Long-stemmed dried naturals, arranged for a bundled appearance, create an attractive wall accent. Ideal for filling a narrow wall space, wall bundles can also be grouped together for larger displays.

This arrangement works well using long-stemmed grains, grasses, or flowers. Choose a dried natural in a texture or color that blends with the decorating scheme. Then use a trim, such as paper twist, rope, raffia, or ribbon, for embellishing the bundle.

MATERIALS

- Dried naturals, such as barley, lavender, rye, roses, or delphinium.
- Decorative trim, such as paper twist, rope, raffia, or ribbon.
- Styrofoam®, 2" (5 cm) thick; serrated knife.
- Heavyweight corrugated paper.
- Cardboard; masking tape.
- 14" (35.5 cm) length of 18-gauge floral wire, for hanger.
- 22-gauge or 24-gauge paddle floral wire; wire cutter.
- Low-temperature glue gun and glue sticks.
- Embellishments, such as dried leaves and artificial berries or grape clusters.

HOW TO MAKE A WALL BUNDLE

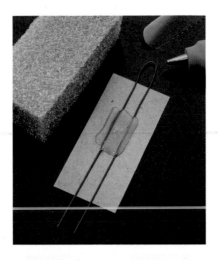

1 Cut Styrofoam to the desired width, using serrated knife; cut the height of the Styrofoam to about 4" (10 cm). Cut one 2" × 4" (5 × 10 cm) piece of cardboard. Bend floral wire in half, and glue it to cardboard, with looped end of wire extending about 1" (2.5 cm) beyond cardboard as shown.

2 Apply glue generously to the wire side of cardboard; center, and secure to back side of Styrofoam. Cut a 6" (15 cm) strip of corrugated paper to wrap around front and sides of Styrofoam and extend to back. Secure corrugated paper to Styrofoam with glue.

3 Glue a piece of cardboard, cut to same size as Styrofoam back, over back of base for reinforcement. Bend ends of wire around cardboard; cover the ends of wire with masking tape.

4 Glue a single layer of stems to corrugated paper, evenly covering the front and sides; center the stems lengthwise on base.

5 Layer additional stems over the previous layer. Wrap wire around base and stems; twist to secure, leaving slack for adjusting the placement of stems. Adjust placement of stems for even distribution and desired height.

6 Wrap second piece of wire around bundle, positioning the wire at the desired location for trim; secure tightly. Remove first wire. Apply glue along wire to prevent any slippage of the stems.

7 Trim ends of stems straight across or at an angle, using scissors. Tie or glue desired trim around bundle, concealing wire and glue. Secure embellishments to front of bundle with glue.

Decorative
Shelves

WALL BOXES

These versatile wall boxes are a unique alternative to traditional shelves. Simple to construct, they can also be made to support glass shelves for an open curio case. Use them in groupings, alone, or displayed with other wall decorations.

Depending on the paint or stain applied, the boxes can be finished in a variety of looks. Paint the inside and outside of the boxes to match the wall. Or, for contrast, paint or stain the back piece of the box to coordinate with the items displayed within the box.

Wall boxes can be made in any size and depth, using ½" (1.3 cm) plywood, hardwood, or medium-density fiberboard, often referred to as MDF. For wall boxes constructed with plywood, purchase grade AA plywood with a veneer finish on both sides. For best results, paint, rather than stain, the laminated edges of the plywood.

Determine the desired dimensions of the wall box, taking into consideration the display size and the finished size of the box. The outside dimensions of the box will be 1" (2.5 cm) larger than the display opening, and the finished depth of the box will be 1¼" (3.2 cm) deeper than the display depth, because the boxes are constructed with a recessed back.

Glass supply stores will cut glass for shelves. Measure for the glass after the shelf is assembled, allowing about ⅛" (3 mm) ease at the sides of the box; the depth of the glass should also be about ⅛" (3 mm) shorter than the display depth of the box.

HOW TO MAKE A WALL BOX

MATERIALS

- ½" (1.3 cm) plywood in AA grade, hardwood, or medium-density fiberboard.
- 1 × 3 lumber, for mounting rail.
- Scraps of 1 × 2 lumber.
- Glass shelves and ¼" × ¾" (6 mm × 2 cm) pine or oak screen molding, for glass supports, optional.
- 16 × 1½" (3.8 cm) brads.

- Wood glue; wood filler.
- Paint or stain, for desired wood finish.
- Jigsaw or circular saw.
- Drill and 1/16" and 1/8" drill bits.
- #8 drywall screws.
- Plastic wall anchors or toggles.
- 220-grit and 80-grit sandpaper and sanding block.

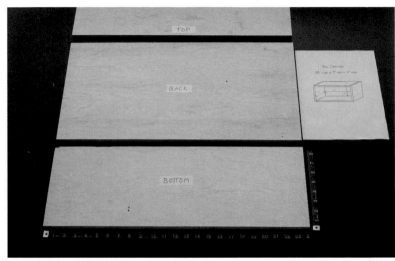

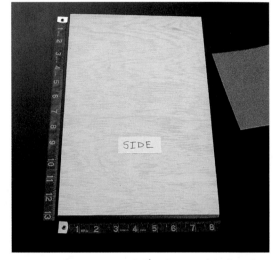

1 **Wall box.** Cut back piece of shelf to correspond to the dimensions of the box opening, or display area. Cut top and bottom pieces with length of pieces equal to length of back piece; depth of the pieces is equal to the desired display depth plus 1¼" (3.2 cm).

2 Cut side pieces with height equal to height of back piece plus twice the thickness of the wood plus scant 1/16" (1.5 mm); cut to same depth as top and bottom pieces. Sand surfaces of wood pieces as necessary.

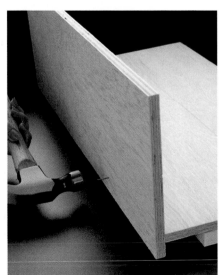

3 Place back piece on 1 × 2 boards to raise the back piece ¾" (2 cm). Apply glue sparingly to upper edge of back piece. Position top piece upright against the glued edge, aligning ends.

4 Predrill nail holes 1" (2.5 cm) from back edge of the board, using 1/16" drill bit; position the holes 1" (2.5 cm) from ends and at 4" to 6" (10 to 15 cm) intervals. Secure with brads; set brads, using a nail set.

5 Repeat steps 3 and 4 to secure the bottom piece. Secure side pieces in place with glue and brads; center the sides so ends are slightly offset, and position the nails at ends about ½" (1.3 cm) from front and back edges.

6 Sand upper edges of the side pieces flush with top piece of the box, using 80-grit sandpaper on a sanding block. Sand the top of shelf using 220-grit sandpaper. Repeat for the bottom of box.

7 Sand front and back edges of box, as needed. Fill the nail holes with wood filler; sand the edges smooth. If using plywood, fill the edges of top, bottom, and side pieces; sand smooth.

8 Paint or stain the box as desired.

9 Cut 1 × 3 lumber to the width of the back board plus about 8" (20.5 cm); mark a line 1" (2.5 cm) from one long edge. Mark board for finished length of the mounting rail with length equal to width of back board less ½" (1.3 cm).

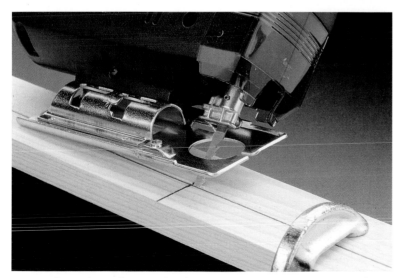

10 Adjust plate of jigsaw for 45° cut. Clamp board to work surface. Cut along the marked line at 45° angle, cutting just beyond the marked stop line. Turn the jigsaw off, and lift out the blade.

11 Readjust jigsaw blade for 90° cut; crosscut the board on the marked line.

(Continued)

12 Lightly sand sharp angled edges of mounting rail pieces to dull edges. Glue narrow strip of mounting rail to bottom of top piece of box, at back of shelf, with angled edge to back of box as shown.

13 Mark remaining mounting rail piece for two screws; position the screws to align with wall studs, if possible. Mark position on wall for mounting rail piece, using a carpenter's level and pencil; angled edge of the mounting rail faces the wall. Upper edge of the mounted wall box extends about ½" (1.3 cm) above the rail.

14 Predrill holes at placement marks on mounting rail, using ⅛" drill bit. Reposition mounting rail on wall, and mark placement of screws on the wall; drill holes for the screws. If there is not a wall stud at the placement mark, install plastic wall anchors or toggles into the drilled holes, using a hammer. Reposition mounting rail on wall, aligning screw holes. Secure rail to the wall using drywall screws.

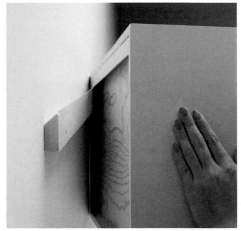

15 Mount wall box on mounting rail.

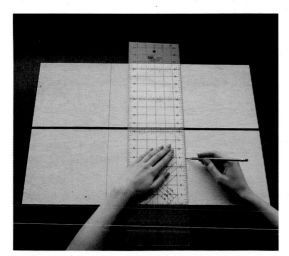

1 **Wall box with shelves.** Follow page 110, steps 1 and 2. Align the side pieces; using straightedge and pencil, mark lines for the position of shelves, taking care to mark lines perpendicular to the front edges of side pieces.

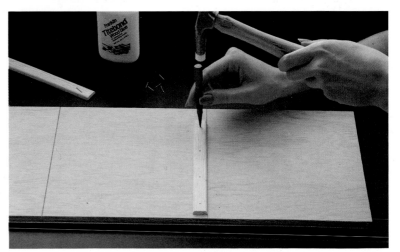

2 Cut molding strips to display depth of box less ⅜" (1 cm); sand ends. Align molding strips with the marked lines, ¼" (6 mm) from front edge; secure in place with glue and ½" (1.3 cm) brads. Set brads with nail set; fill holes with wood filler. Complete box as on pages 110 to 112, steps 3 to 15; insert glass shelves.

MORE IDEAS FOR WALL BOXES

Picture frame molding *is applied to a wall box for a traditional look. The box is lined with wallcovering to complement the plate; apply the wallcovering with wallcovering adhesive.*

Double-door curio cabinet *(above) is made by hinging shutters to a wall box. Select the shutters; then construct the wall box to fit the dimensions of the shutters.*

Display ledges *(left) are made by hanging wall boxes with the open side against the wall. The boxes are constructed like those on pages 110 to 112, but the back piece is not offset. The depth of the top and bottom pieces is equal to the desired display depth.*

Glue narrow mounting rail to inside edge of box as shown.

Simple in style, these tiered shelves make attractive display ledges for curios. The shelves can be made in two heights for a taller, mantel-style shelf or a shorter, gallery-style shelf. If desired, a rail can be added to the shelf for displaying decorative plates.

Poplar, sometimes referred to as aspen, is used for this project because it has minimal warpage. It is also available in several stock sizes, reducing the cutting required for the tiered effect. Purchase the boards in 2' or 3' (61 or 91.5 cm) lengths, depending on the desired shelf length. Or cut the boards to the desired length for a custom-size shelf. The finished height of the shelf is 7" (18 cm) for a mantel-style shelf or 5" (12.5 cm) for a gallery-style shelf. The display depth of both shelf styles is 3½" (9 cm).

The shelves may be finished with paint or stain to complement the decorating scheme. When gluing the boards together, take care to remove any excess glue, using a damp sponge; stain will not penetrate glued surfaces.

MATERIALS

- Two ½ × 2 poplar boards, in desired length.
- Two ½ × 4 poplar boards, in desired length.
- One ½ × 6 poplar board, in desired length, for mantel-style shelf; or one ½ × 4 poplar board, in desired length, for gallery-style shelf.

- ¼" (6 mm) square dowel, for optional rail.
- Scrap lumber about 3⁄16" (4.5 mm) thick, such as pine lath, for spacer strips.
- 16 × 1½" (3.8 cm) brads; nail set.
- Wood glue; clamps.

- Wood filler.
- 220-grit sandpaper.
- Jigsaw or circular saw.
- Drill and 1⁄16" drill bit.
- Paint or stain; two sawtooth picture hangers.

HOW TO MAKE A TIERED SHELF

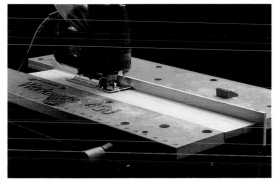

1 Mark line, using pencil, on ½ × 4 board 1¼" (3.2 cm) from long edge. Cut on marked line using jigsaw or circular saw. Board with 1¼" (3.2 cm) depth is upper tier at bottom of shelf; board with 2¼" (6 cm) depth is middle tier at top of shelf.

2 Place the ½ × 6 or the ½ × 4 board for back board of shelf on 3⁄16" (4.5 mm) spacer strips. Apply the glue sparingly to lower edge of back board. Position upper tier for bottom of shelf upright against glued edge, aligning ends. Apply wood glue to the bottom of tier; position ½ × 2 board upright against the glued surface.

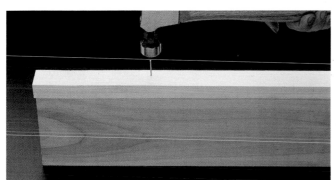

3 Predrill nail holes a scant ½" (1.3 cm) from back edge of board, using 1⁄16" drill bit; position holes 1" (2.5 cm) from the ends and at 4" to 6" (10 to 15 cm) intervals. Secure with brads; set brads, using nail set.

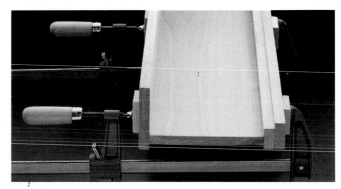

4 Apply glue to upper edge of the back board. Position the ½ × 4 board upright against glued edge, aligning ends. Secure with brads as in step 3. Clamp assembled unit together, using scraps of lumber to protect shelf. Allow glue to dry.

(Continued)

5 Glue the two remaining boards together, aligning the back edges and ends. Apply glue to upper side of board for middle tier and back edges of both boards; secure boards to the back board and underside of upper shelf. Clamp upper shelf tiers in place, using scraps of lumber to protect shelf. Allow glue to dry.

6 Cut plate rail, if desired, by cutting a ¼" (6 mm) square dowel to the length of shelf. Apply wood glue to the bottom of dowel. Secure the dowel to top of shelf, 2" (5 cm) from the back edge. Clamp in place, using a scrap of lumber to protect the rail; allow glue to dry.

7 Fill nail holes with wood filler; sand them smooth. Sand the ends and front of shelf. Paint or stain the shelf as desired.

8 Secure a sawtooth hanger to the recessed back of shelf at each end, positioning the hangers the same distance from the upper edge of shelf.

MORE IDEAS FOR TIERED SHELVES

Wood medallions *are glued to the back board of the shelf; a wood molding embellishes the upper edge of the shelf. For a contrasting finish on medallions and moldings, wipe with white paint and allow to dry before securing to the shelf.*

Shelf with tiered ends *is constructed following the same method as on pages 115 and 116. The lengths of the boards are adjusted for the staggered effect before assembling the shelf.*

Cutouts embellish the back board of the shelf. Drill holes at the corners of each design so a jigsaw blade can be inserted for easy cutting.

RUSTIC SHELVES

These simple shelves have a rustic, woodland style. Made with brackets cut from branches, they are suitable for country and casual decorating schemes. They can also add a touch of whimsy to contemporary or traditional settings.

The shelf board and back board can be cut to any size, using 1 × lumber. Precision cutting is not necessary; crudely cut shelf boards add charm and style to the shelf. The wood may also be distressed for a weathered look.

For the brackets of the shelf, look for sturdy branches that are relatively straight. Use fallen branches, free of rot or disease. Or allow freshly cut branches to cure at least one month, because fresh branches may shrink in size as they dry, pulling away from the shelf boards.

MATERIALS

- 1 × lumber, such as pine, poplar, or maple, for shelf and back board.
- Small branches, such as birch, about 1½" (3.8 cm) in diameter, for support brackets.
- 8 × 1⅝" (4 cm) drywall screws; brads and nail set.
- Wood glue.
- Paint, or stain and matching putty, for desired wood finish.
- Jigsaw or circular saw; crosscut saw.
- Sawtooth picture hangers; self-adhesive rubber or cork bumpers.
- Drill; 3⁄32" drill bit and drill bit slightly smaller than diameter of brads.
- Hammer, chisel, chain, awl, and 100-grit sandpaper, optional, for distressing wood.
- Aerosol clear acrylic sealer.

HOW TO MAKE A RUSTIC SHELF

1 Cut shelf board to the desired length and depth; cut the back board to the desired length and height. Sand boards. Distress the wood, if desired (page 120). Place shelf board, right side down, on ⅛" to ¼" (3 to 6 mm) spacer strips, such as pine lath; apply glue to one long edge. Position right side of the back board against glued edge, as shown.

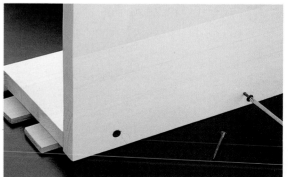

2 Predrill the screw holes ½" to ⅝" (1.3 to 1.5 cm) from the upper edge of back board, using 3⁄32" drill bit; position holes about 2" (5 cm) from ends and at 6" to 8" (15 to 20.5 cm) intervals. Secure with drywall screws.

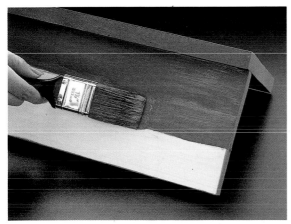

3 Paint or stain the shelf as desired.

4 Cut a strip of paper to the approximate width of the branch. Place end of shelf on the paper as shown; position the paper as desired for the placement of branch support bracket. Mark the paper along the inside edges of wood boards for the angle of cuts; label paper for top and bottom of bracket.

(Continued)

5 Cut paper pattern on marked lines; place on branch, and mark angle of cuts. Cut branch on marked lines. Repeat for any additional brackets.

6 Secure bracket to shelf with brads; predrill holes, using drill bit that is slightly smaller than diameter of brads. Insert brads from top of shelf board and from back of back board, taking care to use brad length that will not penetrate through branch.

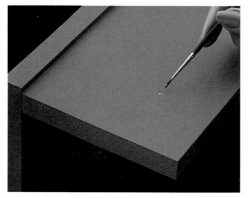

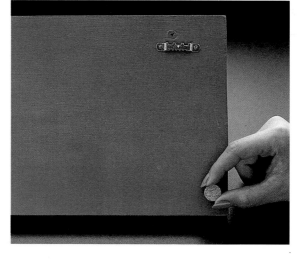

8 Secure sawtooth picture hanger at each end on the back of shelf, positioned about 1" (2.5 cm) from the ends and 1" (2.5 cm) from the upper edge of back board. Secure rubber or cork bumpers at lower corners; layer bumpers as needed to equal depth of sawtooth hangers.

7 Countersink brads on top of the shelf, using a nail set. Fill holes with putty to match the stain, or touch up with paint. Apply aerosol clear acrylic sealer to shelf.

HOW TO DISTRESS WOOD

1 Pound the wood with a hammer, chisel, and chain, and pound holes randomly into wood, using an awl. Make imperfections and dents as desired.

2 Complete the distressed look, chiseling some edges randomly and rounding off edges, using 100-grit sandpaper.

MORE IDEAS FOR RUSTIC SHELVES

Pegs (above), cut from small branches, are inserted into the backing board to create a unique peg rail.

Branch edging (right) trims a small wall shelf. A forked branch extends above the shelf, adding a whimsical touch.

Weathered boards (below) are used in place of new lumber to give the shelf an aged appearance.

CROWN MOLDING
SHELVES

Add architectural detail to rooms with these small wall shelves. Made with decorative crown moldings, they are quick and easy to construct. Use the shelves to accent a small wall space or to add a unique shape to a grouping of framed artwork.

Many building centers stock decorative millwork in a variety of styles. Or they can order it from manufacturers' molding catalogs. For the quickest construction, purchase a mid crown corner molding. This one-piece unit is assembled with three finished sides. Or purchase two outside crown corner moldings, and glue them together to make a shelf.

To avoid a visible center front seam on shelves assembled with outside crown corners, paint, rather than stain, this style shelf. For a painted finish without brush marks, apply an aerosol enamel paint.

The instructions for the mid crown corner molding shelf include a cove molding beneath the shelf ledge. Depending on the style of crown molding selected, this trim may not be necessary.

Crown molding shelves can be made using one mid crown corner molding (*a*) or two outside crown corner moldings (*b*).

HOW TO MAKE A CROWN MOLDING SHELF

MATERIALS

- One mid crown corner molding or two outside crown corner moldings.
- Scrap piece of 1 × lumber, for shelf ledge.
- Scrap piece of ¼" to ½" (6 mm to 1.3 cm) lumber, and decorative molding, for bottom of outside crown corner molding shelf.
- ¾" (2 cm) cove molding, miter box and backsaw, optional, for mid crown corner molding shelf.
- 17 × 1" (2.5 cm) brads; nail set.
- Wood glue; wood filler; paint or stain.
- Jigsaw or circular saw; drill and drill bit.
- Two small sawtooth picture hangers.
- Decorative wood medallion, for mid crown corner molding shelf.

1 **Mid crown corner molding.** Miter cove molding strips for the sides of the crown molding at the front corners, cutting 45° angles; leave excess length on moldings. Miter one corner on the molding strip for the front of shelf, leaving excess length; mark the finished length and angle of miter cut at opposite end. Cut the miter.

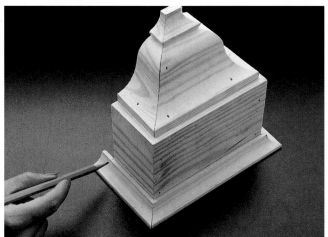

2 Reposition front and side molding strips at the corners. Mark finished lengths of side pieces for straight-cut ends at back edge of crown molding. Set aside molding strips.

3 Cut 1 × lumber to desired size for shelf ledge, allowing 1" to 3" (2.5 to 7.5 cm) overhang at front and sides of crown molding; ledge should be flush at back of shelf.

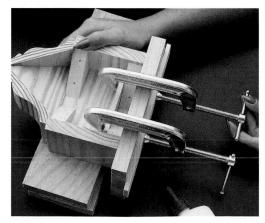

4 Glue shelf ledge to top of crown molding, with back edges flush. Clamp in place, using scraps of lumber to protect shelf; allow glue to dry.

5 Measure the width and depth of back opening in the crown molding below the support braces; cut a piece of scrap lumber, with depth ¼" (6 mm) less than the depth of the opening. This board is mounting board for securing the sawtooth picture hangers. Glue mounting board to the inside support braces; clamp as shown.

6 Apply wood glue sparingly to cove moldings; position around crown molding at underside of the shelf. Predrill nail holes, and secure the molding with brads; set brads, using a nail set.

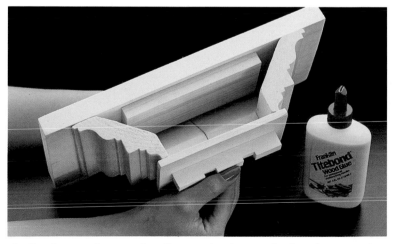

7 Sand the shelf as necessary. Glue decorative wood medallion to shelf, if desired. Fill nail holes with wood filler; sand lightly. Paint or stain the shelf as desired.

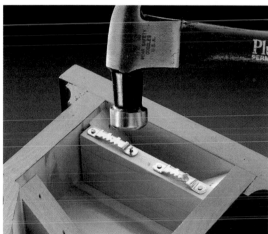

8 Secure a sawtooth hanger at each end of the mounting board at the back of shelf as shown.

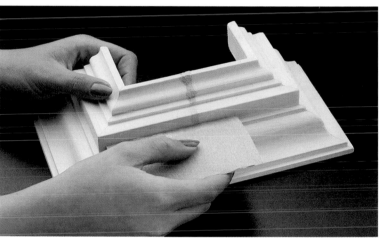

1 **Outside crown corner moldings.** Glue corner pieces together, taking care to align edges at center front; clamp together until glue is dry. Apply wood filler as necessary; sand butted edges smooth.

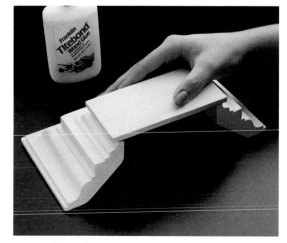

2 Cut base for bottom of the shelf, using scrap lumber ¼" to ½" (6 mm to 1.3 cm) thick. Back edge of base should be flush with back of molding; sides and front edge can be flush or extend slightly. Glue base to the bottom of the molding unit.

3 Continue as in steps 3 to 5 opposite; in step 5, glue the mounting piece to the bottom of the shelf ledge. Cut decorative molding for embellishing bottom of base to desired length. Secure the molding to the base with glue; allow to dry. Sand shelf, if necessary. Paint shelf as desired. Complete as in step 8.

INDEX

CREDITS

CY DECOSSE INCORPORATED

Chairman/CEO: Bruce Barnet
Chairman Emeritus: Cy DeCosse
President/COO: Nino Tarantino
Executive V. P./Editor-in-Chief:
  William B. Jones

PICTURE-PERFECT WALLS
Created by: The Editors of
  Cy DeCosse Incorporated

Also available from the publisher:
*Bedroom Decorating, Creative Window
Treatments, Decorating for Christmas,
Decorating the Living Room; Creative
Accessories for the Home, Decorating
with Silk & Dried Flowers, Decorating
the Kitchen, Decorative Painting,
Decorating Your Home for Christmas,
Decorating for Dining & Entertaining,
Decorating with Fabric & Wallcovering,
Decorating the Bathroom, Decorating
with Great Finds, Affordable Decorating*

Group Executive Editor: Zoe A. Graul
Editorial Manager: Dawn M. Anderson
Project Manager: Elaine Johnson
Assistant Project Manager: Amy Berndt
Associate Creative Director:
  Lisa Rosenthal
Art Director: Stephanie Michaud
Writer: Lori Ritter
Editor: Janice Cauley
Researcher/Designer: Michael Basler
Researcher: Lori Ritter
Sample Production Manager: Carol Olson
Senior Technical Photo Stylist:
  Bridget Haugh

Technical Photo Stylists: Sue Jorgensen,
  Nancy Sundeen
Styling Director: Bobbette Destiche
Project Stylists: Christine Jahns, Coralie
  Sathre, Joanne Wawra
Prop Stylist: Michele Joy
Prop Assistant/Shopper: Margo Morris
Lead Artisan: Carol Pilot
Artisans: Arlene Dohrman, Sharon
  Ecklund, Phyllis Galbraith, Valerie Hill,
  Kristi Kuhnau, Virginia Mateen,
  Ginger Mountin, Carol Pilot, Michelle
  Skudlarek, Nancy Sundeen
*Vice President of Development Planning
  & Production:* Jim Bindas
Director of Photography: Mike Parker
Creative Photo Coordinator:
  Cathleen Shannon
Studio Manager: Marcia Chambers
Lead Photographer: Mark Macemon
Photographers: Rebecca Hawthorne,
  Kevin Hedden, Rex Irmen, William
  Lindner, Paul Najlis, Charles Nields,
  Mike Parker, Greg Wallace
Contributing Photographers: Phil
  Aarrestad, Kim Bailey, Doug
  Cummelin, Paul Englund, Mark Hardy,
  Brian Holman, Steve Smith
Print Production Manager: Patt Sizer
Desktop Publishing Specialist:
  Laurie Kristensen
Production Staff: Deborah Eagle, Kevin
  Hedden, Jeanette Moss, Mike Schauer,
  Greg Wallace, Kay Wethern
Shop Supervisor: Phil Juntti
Scenic Carpenters: Jon Hegge, Troy
  Johnson, Rob Johnstone, John Nadeau
Consultants: Joel Barkley, Suzanne
  Gilbert, Patrick Kartes, Robin Keck
Contributors: Bombay Company; Crescent
  Matboard·Co.; Macy's

Sources for Product Information: Wall
sconces, pp. 5, 14—Fabby Lighting,
450 South La Brea Avenue, Los Angeles,
CA 90036, (213) 939-1388; Copper
Verdigris Solution/Patina Green, pp. 71,
73—MODERN OPTIONS, 2325 3rd
Street, #339, San Francisco, CA 94107,
(415) 252-5580
Contributing Artists: Phil Aarstad,
pp. 15, 27, 85, 86; Jorge Añón, p. 15;
Craig Blacklock, Cover, pp. 8, 9, 36,
39, 40, 54, 68, 69, 76, 77; Camilla
Charnock, p. 114; Kathy Cooney, p. 70;
Bobbette Destiche, pp. 7, 29, 50; Ross
Destiche, p. 7; Bruce Duykers, p. 78;
Gretchen Duykers, pp. 80, 81; Alexandra
Emmons, p. 46; Jane Evershed, pp. 22,
79, from *More Than a Tea Party* by
Jane Evershed © 1994 Jane Evershed,
reprinted by arrangement with Harper
Collins, San Francisco; Elisabeth Fall,
pp. 11, 23; Zoe Graul, p. 6; Bridget
Haugh, p. 29; Christine Jahns, p. 76;
Sue Jorgensen, pp. 4, 74, 75, 113;
Brianne Macemon, p. 82; Mike Parker,
Cover, pp. 2, 32, 44, 50, 83; Chad A.
Peterson, p. 61; Lisa Rosenthal, p. 79;
Larry Sobaskie, pp. 16, 22, 23, 71; Paul
Wawra, p. 83; Sharon Wawra, p. 83;
John Wawrzonek, pp. 68, 82; Abigail
Wyckoff, Cover, pp. 2, 32, 33, 51
Printed on American paper by:
Litho Inc. (1195)

Cy DeCosse Incorporated offers
a variety of how-to books. For
information write:
  Cy DeCosse Subscriber Books
  5900 Green Oak Drive
  Minnetonka, MN 55343